D0729650

WHEN YOUR CANARY QUITS SINGING

A Dictionary of Wholesome Living

TIMOTHY J. UHLMANN, PH.D.

TJU PUBLISHING
Topinabee, Michigan

© 2005 Timothy J. Uhlmann, Ph.D.

Front cover painting © 2005 Dennise Piché

All rights reserved. No part of this book may be reproduced or transmitted in any form or by any means, electronic or mechanical, including photocopying, recording, or by any information storage and retrieval system, without permission in writing from the publisher.

ISBN-13: 978-0-9762934-0-8
ISBN-10: 0-9762934-0-4

Publisher's Cataloguing-in-Publication Data
Uhlmann, Timothy, J.
  When your canary quits singing: a dictionary of wholesome living /
  Timothy J. Uhlmann. — Topinabee, Mich. : TJU Publishing, 2005.

p. ; cm.

Includes index.
ISBN 0-9762934-0-4

1. Conduct of life. 2. Quality of life. 3. Spirituality. 4. Health.
5. Mental Health. I. Title.
BJ1595 .U45 2005   2004099773
170/.44—dc22   0504

Printed in the United States of America
10 9 8 7 6 5 4 3 2 1

Cover and interior design by To The Point Solutions
www.tothepointsolutions.com

To Gloria

CONTENTS

ACKNOWLEDGMENTS

WHEN SOMEONE PUBLISHES FOR THE FIRST TIME, especially at a late state in his career like I am, necessarily he is standing on the shoulders of many mentors, coaches, teachers, and friends. To mention everyone, while desirable, would not be practical. I offer the following, to recognize those who have contributed most directly to the writing of this book.

Thank you to my parents: my mother, Jane, who taught me many lessons, including "Don't cross that bridge before you get to it;" and my dad, Bernard, whose courage probably saved my life the day I pushed over the hornets' tree. I can still see him bravely swatting the angry insects with his hat. Awesome!

Thank you to my wife, Gloria, who by believing I could, and not disturbing my unsightly piling system, encouraged me and unselfishly did not compete for the time it takes to write a book, which was a great deal longer than we had envisioned.

Thank you to my children, Krista and Ben, who did without their dad, while still in high school, when I went searching for the truth at Jungian institutes in Chicago and Detroit, and whose pride in my pursuit of a Ph.D. wouldn't let me disappoint and helped keep me going.

Thank you to my mentors and friends who affirmed my quest: Ed King, Jo Greene, Richard Beachnau, Mike Hardy, Bill Rabior, Bea Reed, Dr. Mary Loomis, Sister Laura Smith, Michael Fonseca, Sister Nancy Brousseau, Judy Hahn, Fr. Richard W. Kropf, Sister Virginia Stasium, Dana C., Bonnie M., Mary B., Kathy M., Kerri E., Jan C., Dale S., and Kathy Sullivan.

Thank you to my teachers: Clark Moustakas, who taught me how to see the truth; Sister Thedeus, RSM, the first teacher to really see me; Prof. Harvey Bercher; Cereta Perry, and Dr. Bruce Douglass.

Thank you to my coach, Dave Woodcock.

Thank you to the students and clients who taught my heart how to sing.

Thank you to Mary Ann Carey and Lori Davis, who endured the brain numbing, induced by transcribing my original handwritten version, written on seemingly endless numbers of legal pads.

Thank you to Dr. Steve Sheridan, Carol O'Connor, JoAnn Fury, Laina Goeke, Sister Jean Umlor, Rosemary Mullaney, Barb Edison, and Sue Patrick. They are commended for reading the first rough draft and making suggestions that led to a much more cohesive version and helped guide the work of editor Mary Jo Zazueta.

Thank you to the Universe, with whom I have a covenant, love, trust, and obey. It is no accident that my name is Temo

Theus and that I was born at noon as the Angelus was ringing and that the first book I ever read was Lives of the Saints, and that I eventually became a soul doctor (psyche-ologist).

And finally, thank you to Thomas Merton for "spilling his guts." After reading his writing I realized if he can strive to become an enlightened one, so can I.

INTRODUCTION

I AM A THERAPIST WITH TRAINING IN SOCIAL WORK AND psychology. After giving my exclusive attention to thousands of clients, one hour at a time, for more than thirty years, I can now point people in the direction of wellness.

In part, this book was written as a response to clients' questions about the distinctive way I sometimes talk during our sessions. It was also written to make several points regarding wholesome living and sustained wellness. One of my intents is to empower and encourage individuals in toxic environments to "Get the hell out of there!"

I do not petition, "Please, consider leaving." Instead I boldly pronounce, "When your canary dies . . . pack your bags and GO!"

Pithiness is sometimes misunderstood and misinterpreted as brutal, too honest, or not gentle enough for sensitive readers. More than a few people will not be ready for this dictionary of wholesome living. If you find that to be the case, my advice is for you to put the book on a shelf or get it out of the house, especially if your canary quits singing.

This book is not meant to offend. However, no attempt has been made to make it neutral, politically correct, subtle, tactful, indirect, non-cutting, or salving.

When Your Canary Quits Singing is a guide to wellness and wholesome living. Like a dictionary, the entries are organized in alphabetical order—not in order of importance. This book can be read from A to Z; but it's okay to randomly select entries to read, and then continue flipping through the pages until you gain a meaningful understanding of wholesome living.

Pick any word to start and then page through the book. Or look for words and issues that are dear to you. Allow for the play of serendipity and synchronicity. The Universe wanted this book written; I received the assignment.

If you love others and see that the path they are on is taking them away from wellness, then it is a good thing to call out to them and to admonish: "Friend! Oh, my! You have chosen a difficult path." If that is preaching, so be it. "What does it benefit a man traversing a rocky path to hold a light behind?"

This is a book about virtue and values, from the voice of experience as heard by a rural psychologist, with a healthy dose of spirituality added.

I am not a theologian, biblical scholar, or comparative religion authority. If this book sounds religious or preachy, it is because my focus is on the nature of humans; and one aspect of human nature is that it is religious.

WHEN YOUR CANARY QUITS SINGING

ABIDE

Humans suffer. The Universe seemingly sends suffering by design. Knowing when to flee and when to persevere requires wisdom. It has been said that suffering that doesn't kill people leaves them stronger or better—more prepared in some way—often for challenges or missions that no one foresees.

Abide is associated with patience, tolerance, and perseverance—traits that make a positive contribution to wholesome living, especially when life gets tough, which it will.

Quitters quit. When the going gets rough they don't endure, they bail out. You don't want these people on your team because when the showdown comes they won't be present. It would be hard to convince the immature that much suffering is meaningful. They feel miserable and only want their misery to stop, which is understandable.

Wholesome living does not require abiding the arrogance of another, especially when it results in unnecessary risk and/or injury to someone.

ACCEPTANCE

If you are in acceptance of what is, you may see God's creation manifesting. And that is a beautiful thing.

The reality is we often don't trust Mother Nature as God created her. Instead of honoring, revering, and laughing with the author (God), we want to re-write the book. When our egos mess with nature, all hell breaks loose. We can't leave good enough alone. We have to tweak it. We think we can improve upon what God created rather than live in acceptance, enthusiasm, and joy.

Advances in science are great but the reality is *we haven't made anything new yet*. We make discoveries of what is hidden and we take what we find and make interesting combinations, some of which are of great benefit to wholesome living and wellness.

We don't create from nothing—we put two and two together and come up with some novelty, like the computer. Such so-called advances (progress) impress our egos; but the reality is there is nothing new under the sun. There is only one creator—we should be in acceptance of His gifts.

ACCOMMODATE

Wholesome relationships and marriages have, at their essence, the willingness of two people to respect and accommodate each other. In order to accommodate, you need to heed what the other person says. Giving the other what you want him/her to have or what you think he/she needs is not accommodating—it is patronizing.

To accommodate in a wholesome way requires truly listening, i.e., when someone says they need space, you must give them space independent of your fears or what you think is in their best interests.

Even if you interpret "I need space" as "This is the first stage of him/her leaving me," to accommodate means you give him/her the space without abuse, invective, or scurrility. Accommodation is not served hot. It should be given quietly and calmly—and in a spirit of acceptance, not resignation.

Accommodation does not contain acquiescence. It contains true acceptance and is without protest. It is with understanding and agreement—and, if possible, with approval.

ACHIEVEMENT

Achievement is the result of promises kept and potential realized. It is not the accumulation of wealth or status. To egocentrically and narcissistically set out to become a millionaire by the age of fifty so you can retire and live in decadence means emotional wellness could only occur incidentally.

That is not achievement. The wealth you accumulate on earth will be left on earth.

Love, however, will follow you anywhere.

Consider carefully what you want to achieve.

ADMIRE

Admire means "to regard with admiration, to think highly of another;" thus it has a one up (the object of admiration) and a one down (the person doing the admiring) quality. If you use another person's positive traits and accomplishments to discount your own traits and accomplishments it is unhealthy.

The "mir" in admiration comes from the Latin word *mirari*, which means mirror. Sometimes when you say, "I admire you" it means "I see myself in the mirror that you are and I like what I see." Many instances of falling in love are like this. You fall in love with yourself as passively reflected by the other person. Often such relationships don't last. It is mere vanity and no good or wellness will come of it.

To not understand projection and reflection is to risk getting caught up in hurtful relationships. Better to be conscious and know yourself. Instead of passively carrying someone else's projections say, "I only wish I was who you say I am. But I know myself well, and what you say doesn't fit. What you must be seeing is the love you are reflected by me. It is not who I know myself to be."

Find someone and love him/her. They don't need to deserve it. "I admire you" should mean "The divinity in me salutes and marvels at the divinity in you." It should mean the strengths you see in an-other are similar to yours, thus you can healthfully say, "I admire you" or "Namaste."

ADVERSARINESS

Not all controversy can or need be avoided. It is unwholesome to be wishy-washy, uncommitted, or spineless. What we resist persists. What we repress, we will sooner or later address, so it is better to be bold about issues than to remain neutral. This is the most direct route to the truth.

Most of us will be more likely to hear the truth if it is presented by a peaceful messenger. Most will struggle to hear the truth if it is presented by a snorting, rumbling, menacing bulldozer. Jane Pauley once said, "Nothing thrives in a pressure cooker."

Canaries quit singing around belligerent types. If your canary quits singing because you are exposed to a pressured, urgent person, get the hell out of there.

If you are a belligerent, adversarial person who is always mired in contestations, there is something more than simple rebellion going on. Wellness will stay out of reach until you discover, like St Francis, what you are doing wrong.

ADVENTURE

Have you noticed that people who like a lot of things—colors, textures, shapes, movement, patterns, themes, the first crack of dawn, rainy Sundays, Monday morning, sunrises, dandelion wine, etc.—are interesting? While negative, critical, jaundiced pessimists, devoid of enthusiasm, are avoided like the plague?

If you want to be an interesting person, sample life and find things to do and enjoy.

Just like U-Haul advertises "Adventures in Moving," make your life a series of *adventures in living*. When an adventure is completed, consider it a pearl and place it on a string. Once you've acquired many strings of pearls you'll be an interesting person.

When you have adventure in your life, you won't envy others' pearls. Instead you will admire these people and be able to trade stories about your respective experiences.

Additionally, people who have lived well and have completed many adventures—while perhaps wanting more time to add a few more pearls—do not fear death.

Indeed, dying well is their final adventure. They are awake and pay attention when death comes. They don't want to miss out on any aspect of this seemingly final pearl.

Thus, the way to not worry about dying is to live one moment at a time. While the past and future are relevant, it is most important to pay attention to the moment you are in.

AGGRESSION

The essence of aggression is will, initiative, and non-passivity. Aggression has the potential to do good—but it must be carefully regulated and adjusted for each situation. To be stingy and selective in its use is a balancing act.

It has been said, "Don't use the bomb on Hiroshima when a pea-shooter will do." Too much aggression is dangerous, but too little is unwholesome.

ANIMATE

Animate is from the Greek word *animare*, which means "to give life to;" the Greek word *anemos*, which means "wind;" and the Latin word *anima*, which means "soul."

A wind that gives life to your soul, literally breathes it into you, is what gives you animation.

Carl Jung taught that this spirit was divided into male and female, the animus and anima. "The animus," he said, "was an inner masculine part of the female personality, while the anima was an inner female part of the male personality." The anima and animus are ultimately to be found behind a lot of mischief, especially when they remain unconscious.

ANTICIPATION

Anticipation is associated with intention, direction, volition, possibility, and potential—all of which are essential to wellness. They are at the core of wholesome living. They make the past, present, and future meaningful, seamless, and emergent.

Life is lived moment to moment in the gift of the present. But without anticipation, no one would plant bulbs in the fall for spring flowers. Planting bulbs is an investment of energy, an entrustment of the soil's potential. Burying money is not good stewardship, but when you plant bulbs it is an act of anticipation, love, and trust in emergence and possibility.

Preparation and planting are essential to spirituality. God is the gardener who started time for us and seeded it. To plant and grow is to participate in an important dance. You are like a bulb. You need to prepare and seed yourself with new learning—in anticipation of growth and blossoming.

Potential is love invested. Love realized is a flowering that happens in the present, but it was preceded with anticipation.

The experienced gardener's ability to get things to flower appears magical to those without a green thumb. But there is no trick to it. The successful gardener wonders and anticipates what the bulbs and seeds need.

God has also anticipated your needs. You have everything you need to flourish. But flowering is not automatic. The potential flowering (unfolding love being unfolded by love itself unfolding) is optional. The tree blooms because it is fertilized, hoed, and planted where the sun shines.

A lazy gardener gets the growth that reflects his investment. God is not a lazy gardener but often times *we* are.

Timing and placement aren't everything, but when and where to plant your seeds of potential is important. Watch only successful gardeners. God started time and space for us, but what you do with your life is up to you. You were given intentionality and volition.

The gardener who understands the potential resting in seeds does not plant them on a steep slope. A garden placed there will germinate as the spring rain awakens the seeds, but it will not flourish because the water will run off, leaving the plants needing water. If the next rain is heavy it will wash the seedlings out by their roots.

The gardener listens to the garden not once a month, not once a week, but daily—morning, noon, and night—if he can. His visits become infrequent only when the garden rests during the cold winter months.

Listening alone, however, will not get it done. He has to act, to give the garden what it needs; to protect it from the competition of weeds; and damage from pests, insects, and animals.

APOLOGY

An apology offered quickly and contritely on the heels of an inadvertent offense sets the stage for reconciliation *before* alienation escalates. Typically when we are offended we become defensive, and many people, as a reaction to feeling threatened, act aggressively and offensively. Thus, even a minor unintentional alienating act can result in something like spontaneous combustion, i.e., rapid escalation to rage and fury.

"I'm sorry" can be like baking soda thrown onto a flaming pan of bacon grease. Apology is essential to wholesome living.

Unfortunately lawsuits have made it financially hazardous to apologize, since an apology can be offered as an admission of guilt in court proceedings. Our culture is losing the ability to resolve disputes without retaining attorneys to face off for us like hired guns in the Old West.

APPRECIATE

To appreciate is akin to loving. Loving the experience of life that we are a part of—the sunshine, the rain, a good song, laughter, the quiet in Nature, etc.

To appreciate something or someone, we must pay attention, which is a good thing. Appreciation is a form of grasping something, of "getting it." To be truly appreciated a person or thing must be understood.

Being appreciative grows out of experience. An appreciative person has a better awareness of a person or thing's worth, quality, or significance.

An appreciation for the low-key elements in life can keep the servant leader going when same-age cohorts are becoming millionaires through ruthless capitalism.

Appreciation is challenging, but it brings deeper meaning to your daily experience.

ATTENTION

Attention is essential to enlightenment. If I could only give one piece of advice regarding wellness it would be to pay attention. Each of us is a lamp in front of a mirror; therefore to keep the lamp burning brightly we must have an ample supply of oil and keep the lens and mirror undistorted and clean.

When two people look at each other, each sees him/herself in the mirror that the other is. If you do not pay attention, you will fail to distinguish between your self and the other person—and confusion will ensue. This is why the sage said, "Know thyself." If you don't know who you are, you won't recognize your reflection in the other person and you will think the projection that is you is the other.

The sage also said, "You can see the sliver in your friend's eye but not the beam in your own." Pay attention to the details in your life.

Aspiration

Aspiration means to strive, often for something higher than one's self. It usually implies the striver is ennobled.

If you aspire to trust, love, and obey a higher power, you will be headed in the right direction.

AUDACITY

There is something about bodaciousness that makes people smile. Children have a lot of it, though eventually adults "train" it out of them.

Jesus said, "Unless you become like little children, you will never see the Kingdom of God." He didn't specify certain traits of children, so it seems safe to assume audacity, boldness, and bodaciousness (bold + audacious) will not be deterrents to entering Heaven—while, perhaps, a lack of it will.

"Such audacity!" Only someone who does not understand what is going on here, what this place is, and who we are, is likely to use *audacity* as a pejorative. They take offense where none is intended, standing firmly on the conviction of their superiority and confident in the big deals they make with the power they have accumulated. They are nothing more than arrogant frogs in large ponds. They are nothing in the larger reality. They are Big Shooters only in the illusion. When the dam breaks the big fish and the little minnows get swept away in unison, in the same fashion.

Your rank on the planet doesn't impress God. What will matter is where you rank with Him. The quiet politeness of high civility will be drowned out by the din sent up by the band of saints marching in. You can bet on it.

Go softly most of the time, but realize it is okay to send up a holy din episodically. Don't be so quiet that God has a hard time finding you.

AWE

When awe is combined with dedication, reverence, and honor you will be on the path to wellness. Unfortunately, although many are called, few go because they are alienated by the overly devout.

Devotion is a response to some quality of the object and is a diversion from ongoing awareness of the light that you are. This happens in religion when Jesus is made so sweet and saccharin that he becomes indigestible. When God is portrayed in certain ways, i.e., over-reaching sacredness, many individuals simply conclude He is too high, too distant, too alien, and simply out of reach for them.

That is a misunderstanding of one's simplicity and humility and is the wrong way to go. On the other hand, every time I see one of those "God is my co-pilot" bumper stickers, my canary quits singing. My thought is: "Let God drive and you take the co-pilot seat because your driving is horrible."

There is a balance to be struck between irreverent casualness and off-putting over-elevation and veneration. God doesn't need you to put yourself down in order for Him to stay up. Of course, knees are for kneeling, but too much differential gesturing keeps God at a distance.

Better to remember who you are, have every breath be a prayer, and be a God-inspired driver.

Caution: If someone is in awe of you, be careful. Many romantic notions are merely descriptions of addictions. If somebody proposes being addicted to you as in "I can't live without you," no matter how romantic his or her song sounds, run—don't walk—before your canary stops singing. If somebody "can't breathe without you" your canary will suffocate.

BALANCE

The essence of balance is equilibrium, stability, and consistency. Balance in many things is required if wholesome living is to be attained. Wholesome living involves a balance of solitude and fellowship. There needs to be a balance between work and play. A balance between selfishness and service to others. Of normal narcissism and thoughtful consideration of others. Wholesome living requires a balance between passiveness, aggression, assertiveness, action, and inaction.

Balance is not usually associated with excess. It is difficult to keep excess in balance. Everything in moderation. Even moderation in moderation, i.e., you wouldn't want to stay in the middle all of the time. It is okay to visit the extremes or to say once in a while, "I can't believe I ate the whole thing!" Too much balance can lead to banality and boredom, which is unwholesome.

As a general rule, stay out of drama triangles—love triangles. When it comes to excitement of any kind the "only in moderation rule" is especially important. You *can* get too much of a good thing.

It is better to wish others just enough, as illustrated by the following story that appeared on the Internet (sorry, I do not know the source):

Recently I overheard a father and daughter talking at the airport. Her plane's departure had been announced and they were standing near the security gate as they hugged. The father said, "I love you. I wish you enough."

She said, "Daddy, our life together has been more than enough. Your love is all I ever needed. I wish you enough too, Daddy." They kissed and she left.

He walked toward the window where I was seated. I could see he wanted and needed to cry. I tried not to intrude on his privacy, but he welcomed me in by asking, "Did you ever say good-bye to someone, knowing it would be forever?"

"Yes, I have," I replied. Saying that brought back memories of expressing my love and appreciation for everything my dad had done for me. Recognizing that his days were limited, I took the time to tell him face to face how much he meant to me. So I knew what this man was experiencing.

"Forgive me for asking, but why is this a forever good-bye?" I asked.

"I am old and she lives far away. I have challenges ahead, and the reality is her next trip back will be for my funeral."

"When you were saying good-bye I heard you say, 'I wish you enough.' May I ask what that means?"

He began to smile. "That's a wish that has been handed down from other generations. My parents used to say it to everyone." He paused for a moment and looked up as if trying to remember it in detail. He smiled even more.

"When we said 'I wish you enough,' we were wanting the other person to have a life filled with enough good things to sustain them," he continued. Then he faced me and recited the following from memory:

"I wish you enough sun to keep your attitude bright.
I wish you enough rain to appreciate the sun more.
I wish you enough happiness to keep your spirit alive.
I wish you enough pain so that the smallest joys in life
  appear much bigger
I wish you enough gain to satisfy your wanting.
I wish you enough loss to appreciate all that you possess.
I wish enough hellos to get you through the final good-
  bye."
He began to sob and walked away.

BETRAYAL

In the process of knowing your self and being true to your self you may need to change course. People who assumed you would always do what you did and always be who you were will be flabbergasted when you change. Others, especially a partner, may feel as though you've dropped your end of the pole.

Even when family members realize your departure is a result of being true to a higher calling, a different vocation, or a new self-realization, they experience your leaving as betrayal, abandonment, and hurtful disappointment. Later they may understand that the fact you were consistently the same person for thirty years did not constitute a promise you would be that person for another thirty years.

The right to seize an opportunity, to change and explore an unknown facet of your self, to respond to a vocation to be a missionary in Africa, etc., is not only a constitutional right, it is a God-given right. But knowing that is why you dropped your end of the pole does not make it less jarring for your partner or family when your end strikes the ground.

This sort of betrayal, while unlike its malicious cousin, cheating, is still experienced as hurtful to others and may leave them in dismay and confusion for many years.

Realize that several months or years of alerting your partner to the fact you are going to put your end of the pole down—no matter how gently you set down your end—will do little to lessen the bitterness of their experience of betrayal. This is true to such an extent that it is debatable whether the effort to inflict so much pain *gently* is the correct strategy. It's like when a nurse gives a man with a hairy arm the choice of having the bandage removed one hair at a time or ripped off quickly.

The wound inflicted by betrayal can heal eventually, usually in three to five years. Add cheating, abandonment, conspiracy, character assassination, deceit, and other lowly behaviors to betrayal, and the wound may require a lifetime to heal.

Betray if you must—but otherwise avoid it.

BLISS

Discovering you have a passion for something—writing, art, music, baking, gardening—and then pursuing that aspiration, can bring bliss into your life. People who follow their dreams usually experience good physical and emotional health.

However, don't give up your day job until your passion demonstrates that it can pay the bills. If you follow your bliss too soon, *they* might come and take your furniture.

Finding the middle ground between security and following your bliss is a balancing act.

BONDING

Infant-mother bonding and attachment are essential to the ongoing wellness of the human species (quite frankly, we are screwing up in this department, as evidenced in part by our bulging prison population). The literature on bonding and attachment is encyclopedic and won't be rehashed here.

Infants are born prepared to teach their parents. But they can't do that if the parent isn't available, especially the mother. By making the economy the top priority, as in "It's the economy stupid," we are being insane idiots. Affluence and parental riches cannot replace what is lost when bonding is absent.

Children who missed out on bonding and attachment with their parents are often ticking time bombs. They don't just fade away like old soldiers. Their number continues to grow and they are often homicidal and/or suicidal. Single mothers often must work two jobs to survive. (Forty percent of the boys in this country do not have a father residing at home.)

Ask any adoption worker, adoptee, or adoptive parent involved in a placement in which bonding failed to occur what to expect. The best adoptive parents cannot ameliorate the sense of abandonment and betrayal many adopted children experience (thank God not all do) when considering their histories. These kids wage a life of protest and rebellion. They are often aloof, cannot form attachments with people, and are usually depressed. Many of them are predators that end up in jail.

If the human species does not encourage, potentiate, and support the bond between mothers and their children soon, there is going to be hell to pay.

BOUNDARIES

Boundaries are instrumental to wellness. A solid boundary creates a container for the psyche, whereas fuzzy boundaries are ineffective. (Dysfunctional families are an example of a group with fuzzy boundaries.)

With clear-cut boundaries it is relatively easy to tell where your boundary ends and another's begins, as in "your right to swing your fist ends where my nose begins."

Maintaining boundaries requires an ongoing wellness program; just as maintaining good muscle tone requires regular exercise. One must continually work at keeping boundaries in place.

BUTTERFLY

Butterfly is from the Old English word *butterfleoge* (butter + fly = butterfly), which originated from the belief that witches in butterfly shapes stole milk and butter.

For the Greeks, the butterfly was a symbol for the soul. This is understandable given the butterfly's gossamer insubstantialness. Not only can a butterfly float high on mere zephyrs of wind, it also has the strength to migrate great distances. Of course, all this is preceded by the transformation from caterpillar, a rather slow moving earthbound worm, to winged creature that can climb high and glide on the wind.

Many believe we are sent here by the Universe to go through a metamorphosis, not unlike the butterfly. The mechanisms that land us here and get us out of here are poorly understood at best. We know that, like a pinned butterfly in a museum, a dead human is devoid of his/her essence. It has flown.

Change

Learning to accept change is essential to wellness. Scientists tell us that change was set in motion by the Big Bang when time started and that the Universe continues to expand. The opposite of an expanding Universe is a large black hole. Surrender to the reality of change.

To divide phenomena into things that "can be changed and things that can not be changed" is a gross over-simplification. Everything has to be *accepted as it is*—that has to come first—change or not.

CHEER

The essence of cheer is a gladness that empowers, which is why when we see someone moping, we say, "Cheer up!"

There is no such thing as bad cheer—only good cheer. You can't cheer on someone by hammering on them. It will not cheer up someone if you tell them what they are doing is wrong or you ask, "What is it about this you don't understand?"

To cheer someone you yell, "Have courage!" You applaud them. You yell, "You go, girl!"

CIVILITY

The essence of civility is a thoughtful gentleness that is easy on people's nerves and oftentimes soothing. Anyone with class or elegance has mastered civility. Civility is a discipline. Don't expect to see it in impulsive hotheads or fly-by-the-seat-of-your-pants people.

Civility and humility are not mutually exclusive. In fact, individuals advanced in humility are invariably civil.

The biggest threat to civility is anger. To remain coolly civil while angry requires good breeding and valuing the ethic that holds being polite as a high priority and/or advanced spiritual development.

CLOCK

When God started time for us, he gave us the "clock" of dawn and dusk by causing the Earth to rotate on its axis while orbiting the sun. He gave us the time of the seasons by causing Earth's incline to change relative to the sun over a specific period of time.

This is the only clock we need and the one we should pay attention to. The clocks on our walls and bed stands are dictators. They are helpful when cooking but they impose unnatural rhythms on our days. We don't run our lives by the clock; rather the clock runs us. We have become slaves to the adage, "Time is money."

God didn't create anything that measured nanoseconds. We did. He gave us the moon, which created tides. "Sand flowing through the hourglass" was replaced with "running against the clock" and today's "photo finish" replaced "down to the wire," which will eventually be replaced by even more sophisticated computer-assisted clocks.

When you live "against" the clock you are at war with time itself. That is not the route to a long life.

Take a breath.

Enjoy the day.

COHERENT LIGHT

Coherent light is the laser with which a hologram is made and the light by which it is illuminated. Without coherent light, we are goners.

The light that you are, that Love is, that Jesus said He was, cannot illuminate the hologram if it is inconsistent, unfocused, and scattered about.

When Frenzel lenses beamed bright rays from lighthouses, it was a marvel to see. Marvel means "something that causes wonder or astonishment, intense surprise or interest." Coherent light (a laster beam) is also marvelous; and so-called "laser beamers" are at once marvelous and gifts to the rest of us.

Jesus and Buddha were prototypical laser beamers. With Jesus' help it ought to be easier for us than it was for Buddha. Points of light and sparks of light are good, but they pale in comparison to the coherent light of a laser.

There is light in Heaven and it is coherent light.

COLLABORATION

Collaboration means "to labor together, to walk jointly with others." Someone coined the word *collabatition* (collaboration + competition) to make the point that different entities facing off in a given market can find ways to cooperate and get together rather than compete as non-communicating enemies (or worse, putting out disinformation to confuse the competition).

Lately our government officials have used disinformation for "security reasons," which means they lie to us for "our own good." If another person did this to you, would you ever consider them safe or trustworthy?

Working with others is essential to wellness. Values and virtues do not justify aggression against your enemies or your competition—unless it is to defend your life.

Collaboration is one way of turning the other cheek.

COMFORT

Being able to comfort one's self is essential to wellness. It is a threshold developmental challenge presented in early infancy and remains important throughout life, especially at the end. An infant that can't be calmed is in big trouble and a baby that doesn't learn from caregivers how to calm and comfort him/her self will fail to thrive.

The trouble with comforting *things* (like "comfort food") is that their pleasure is so basic they can easily become addictive. Since we won't need *learned* comforts in Heaven, we will do well to distinguish between spiritual comforts and planetary ones.

If your faith is a comfort, that is a valuable thing, much more so than the numerous psychological defense mechanisms that comfort us by smoke-and-mirror tricks of the ego.

Your journey through life won't always be comfortable, so an important aspect of wellness is learning to do without comfort.

Garrison Keilor said, "Fishing in the rain is a fine and pleasant misery." There are many stretches in the journey that are "fine and pleasant miseries." If traveling in comfort becomes too important, when the going gets rough you may not be tough enough to keep going. Your efforts won't yield results if a little adversity sidetracks you.

Fishing in the rain is good preparation for the labors that are necessary for dream realization.

COMMITMENT

Mit means to send. A commitment is a promise to continue to send something to another person, cause, or organization. The ability to make and keep a commitment is essential to wholesome living.

People are actually freed by commitment. Commitments establish a promise—a covenant—and by adhering to the covenant you can free yourself from yourself.

The inability to be loyal and to keep promises rules out wholesome relationships. The failure to be true to a commitment can devastate the person to whom the commitment was given. Many months, and often years, are required for healing if a personal commitment is broken, especially if it's a marital commitment, which involves a promise to direct certain aspects of one's self only to one's spouse.

COMMUNICATION

The essence of communication is the effective transmission of a message from one person to another. The sent message is received by a listener who, if he/she wishes, can send an acknowledgement. At minimum the acknowledgment lets the sender know the receiver was listening and heard the message. "How do you read me?" "Loud and clear." It doesn't, however, tell the sender if the listener understood the message or got its meaning. Listening is good, but listening without understanding and caring is merely transcription.

The communication of feelings is essential to wholesome living. When the communication of emotions results in affinity and accord, a mutual admiration can ensue, which is invaluable. Rapport between people depends on communication.

CONCERN

The essence of concern is hovering watchful attention. Concern is more effective when it is given with thoughtful attention rather than offered indiscriminately to anyone and everyone.

Concern and care are powerful dynamics that should be evident in all relationships that are important to you.

CONCILIATE

Conciliate means "to gain (as goodwill) by pleasing acts, to make compatible, to soothe, to calm." To be able to change resentment and bitterness to goodwill is to be a soothing refrain, like a lullaby.

It is a gift to ease anger and calm disturbance.

CONDUCT

Conduct means "to act or behave in a particular and especially controlled or directed manner." How you conduct yourself impacts your wellness and the wellness of others.

Years ago there were higher expectations of conduct for adults and children. The lowering of the bar for good conduct has negatively impacted the wellness of society.

CONSISTENCY

Consistency is the essence of reliability and predictability. Someone living a wholesome life is able to make predictions about their behavior and make and keep promises.

No one can become a safe person without first developing the capacity to be consistent. People who can't achieve consistency are unreliable; they often fail to show up for important life events. And worse, when the going gets tough, the inconsistent person will let people down since he/she is unable to do anything in a sustained manner, which rules out staying the course.

Inconsistent people should have a Surgeon General's warning tattooed on their foreheads.

Wholesome living would not be possible if the Universe were totally unreliable and unpredictable.

COURAGE

Courage is love in the midst of fear. It takes courage to run toward danger. Danger and fear can bring about great acts of courage, for example, when a parent sees his/her child in peril and runs to the child's rescue with *no thought* of his/her own safety. There's the clue: The way to courage is "no thought."

Thinking gets in the way of courage, therefore keep thinking to a minimum. It is not "I think therefore I am," rather it is "I am before I have a thought; at this moment I am independent of any thinking; and I will be, even when I have ceased thinking."

If you have to see around every curve in a journey *before* you set out, you'll never venture. The truth will set you free—but you must have courage to find and face the truth of your self.

Wellness is not possible without courage. Don't look outside your self for courage; it's not there. You must look inside.

Courtesy

The essence of courtesy is respect for others, which manifests as civility. The essence of civility is politeness and the absence of rudeness.

A courteous person is not harsh or rude—even when such behavior could be justified by the provocation of others. The courteous person keeps his/her head when everyone else loses theirs (read the poem "If" by John Masefield).

Courtesy and hospitality are characteristics of someone who consistently lives in a wholesome way.

CREATURES

The presence of God's creatures promotes wellness. Need proof? Take a gentle, loving pet into a nursing home and watch the interaction between creature and man. Creatures calm and sustain humans in many ways. Their primary emotions are unconditional love, service, loyalty, trust, and fear. They need our protection like we need protection from the Universe. What a different world this would be if we trusted the Universe like so many of God's creatures trust us.

CRYING

Having a good cry when you need one is essential to wellness. A good cry (and a good laugh) is, through grace, a gift from the Universe.

Crying is the sound of pain. We suffer because the quintessence of this Universe is impermanence. Thus it is that love flows into and out of our lives. Some inexperienced, young, and foolish people might promise us permanence— but to believe them is idolatry.

Crying is the sound of joy. The tears parents shed at the birth of their child and at the child's wedding are chemically distinct from those that flow at funerals. The body knows what it is doing. Some tears hurt. Tears of joy soothe. Tears of anger and rage well up, often unexpectedly, and burn like fire.

Crying is the sound of impermanence. It is the sound of nostalgia; the painful yearning we feel when we realize we can't return to some past time or condition in our lives. With such a realization comes the need to grieve and to cry.

CURIOSITY

Curiosity comes from the Latin word *curiosus*, which means "careful, inquisitive" and from *cura*, which means "cure." Curiosity is a "desire to know" and "interest leading to inquiry." It is a desire to investigate and to learn. Wholesome living, long-term wellness, and perhaps survival of the human species, are closely tied to ongoing learning.

Curiosity needs to be balanced by the ability to Mind Your Own Business (MYOB), i.e., wholesome curiosity is not to be confused with nosiness.

It has been said, "What you can't control is none of your concern." MYOB. Curiosity outside of one's purview (the range or limits of authority, competence, responsibility, concern, or intention) is almost surely meddlesome. The efforts of busybodies masquerading as unsolicited helpers are a vexation to the spirit.

DANCE

Life is a dance. Invite, lead, or follow.
Just don't fail to dance.

DEATH

Jesus demonstrated that the true victory over death is to live without fear, especially without fear of dying. To have trepidation about the manner in which you die is an aspect of not being in denial about death. "Pick up your cross and follow me" means don't let your cross be an anchor.

With your roots in the fertile soil of fear, you can't move. Fearful people are rigid, catatonic. It is fearlessness that allows a healer to move toward the sound of pain, not away from it, and to touch it when he/she arrives, to be a conduit with one finger reaching to touch God's finger, as depicted in Michelangelo's painting, and the other reaching to touch the "leper Christ" in his beggar disguise.

DEDICATION

A person shows dedication when his/her non-action or action is guided by the best interests of a cause, person, enterprise, or activity, continually, in a never-ending cycle.

Dedication requires a high level of awareness and consciousness. Dedication cannot be sustained if the cause, person, activity or enterprise becomes commonplace and over-familiar.

How much dedication is wholesome and reasonable is an individual decision. It is best not solely determined by the neediness of the cause, person, activity, or enterprise. Too much dedication to a too needy cause can lead to exhaustion. The dedicated person is responsible for pacing her/himself.

Wholesome dedication will ebb and flow, wax and wane. A dedicated person's energy is finite. When the dedicated person is at ebb tide, it reflects a phase of energy, just as the moon has phases.

Dedication can ebb and flow with illness, fatigue, distractions, and demanding work. Dedication that excludes too many other things verges on obsessiveness and/or a perfectionist's excess.

Devotion

Devotion, like dedication and love, is something you *are,* not something you *do*. I am devoted. I am dedicated. I am love.

Devotion can be dangerous. It can squander the light that you are. What are the odds that someone (or an organization) can remain worthy of your devotion?

The only way to *do* devotion in a wholesome way is unconditionally. To "do good for nothing." That way, devotion is a statement of who you are. If you give the gift of the light that you are, with no expectations of the other person, when his/her flaws manifest you can smile and say, "Ahhh! Of course." And you can then continue with your devotion, seeing more clearly how needy the recipient is—or you can declare them unworthy and withdraw your devotion.

You are defined by your devotion, not by flawed humans, organizations, or causes. Others will see that your recipients are unworthy. Judging types will deem them unworthy and be puzzled by you, not understanding that your devotion is unconditional and given freely, for no reason. ("She's still

with that alcoholic husband of hers, after twenty-seven years!")

You get to have the experience of what you give away freely. When you shine unconditionally, what you experience, you can keep. No one can take it away. What you try to keep, you lose.

"But I have been hurt so many times!" you declare. Of course you have. So what? Defy your perpetrators and shine anyway. It is the best vengeance. "Yes, but I have not been fed good food. I was not affirmed. Hugs were scarce or nonexistent. I wasn't validated. I came up hard!" Of course you did.

The flowers of aridity are impressive. They bloom without the essentials that more common flowers need. If you can, as the poster says, "Bloom where you are planted now." Those that understand will marvel at you and your bright light will be a precious inspiration. They can think of your devotion and find no excuse for not blooming profusely themselves.

DIFFICULT PEOPLE

Difficult people remind you who you are—and that is essential to long-term wellness. When your love has an object to reflect off of, it is easier to see your love and be reminded of who and what you are. Even difficult people can act as reflecting tools for your love.

Of course, keep your canary with you. If it quits singing, get the hell away from the toxic person. You have worked hard to achieve tranquility. There is no obligation to let difficult people bring you down. The regressions they can cause are painful and when this happens, the community loses the light that you are.

DISCERNMENT

Discern is from the Latin word *discernere*, which means to separate. Discernment is essential to exiting a herd mentality and resisting social pressure to conform. It is much easier to "go along, to get along" than it is to discern and say, "The king has no clothes on."

Discernment is the ability to grasp and comprehend what is obscure. In Christianity, it is said to be one of the gifts of the Spirit [1 Cor 12:1 13]. It is the power to see what is not evident to the average mind. Discernment implies a searching mind that goes beyond what is obvious or superficial, combined with the ability to quickly and sympathetically select what is true, appropriate, or excellent.

Discernment can be practical and realistic. It is the ability to see things as they actually are, and that often does not agree with the so-called consensus reality or dogma of the day. Historically, people gifted with discernment were killed for speaking up about their experiences. Powerful institutions chose to silence discerning individuals rather than suffer through the misery of trying to incorporate a recently uncovered truth. This is why it is important to not pray for serenity or happiness but instead to pray for courage to continue forth on your journey.

If someone discerns that something can be changed but perceives no call to action, preferring to leave good enough alone, that is his business. If someone discerns the intolerable and does nothing, that is idolatry. It wasn't Jesus' power tactics with the politics of His day that got Him in trouble; it was the power tactics of the politicians that He frightened.

Make haste slowly as you live out your song, as traversing the rocky path of discernment is risky business.

DISCOVERY

Discovery is awesome! Without discovery you can't uncover the truth of life. The truth, like sunken treasure, gets covered with layers of silt. If you want the truth you must look for it (see "Adventure") and quite possibly kick up significant dirt in the process.

Adventures in discovery are a lot like hydraulic mining; much soil has to be washed away before the precious minerals are found. Anyone who searches for the truth will move mountains of dirt in the process. And oftentimes, once uncovered, the gems of truth become buried again.

Discovery is a perpetual adventure.

Disengage

Only if you can disengage from your thoughts, your feelings, your body, your mind, and any planetary structures like
time, space, rituals, family, job, national identity, etc., can
you begin to remember who you are.

DOGMA

We are not born into this world with an instruction manual; thus the wise teachings from sages and prophets are important guides for our ascent and continued growth. We can pause to rest—but not for long.

One way to spot your next teacher is to watch for someone who agitates and confuses you. That is likely a person who will occasion new growth and encourage you to reach the next rung on the ladder of life.

Learning to comfort your self is one of the first challenges you have after birth—and it will remain high in the order of business for the rest of your life. If you can't comfort your self at any age with dogma or by some other method, you are in trouble.

However, if this or any book disturbs you so much that you can't comfort your self after reading it, put it down. If it kills your canary, get the book out of the house.

DOING NOTHING

When done correctly, doing nothing can be restorative and help sustain wellness. Doing nothing is particularly satisfying if it's your thing (as in "do your own thing"). If that is the case for you, when you do your own thing, you are doing nothing.

Doing nothing would be considered a luxury or decadent if it didn't have value. Doing nothing may be self-indulgent and given to one's self as an aspect of abundance, like the choice of a superior grade of beef for tonight's steak and premium red wine to go with it.

When you appreciate the value of doing nothing, you would never intentionally interrupt someone who is doing nothing by asking for help, because that would arrest the episode of doing nothing right then and there. If you have to tally up all you've done during the week in order to give yourself permission to do nothing, you are justifying an indulgence that you want but consider sinful, i.e., "I really want to do nothing, but I've got to earn it. For all I do, this doing nothing is for me."

If you consider standing in line at the supermarket or waiting for your ship to come in, as doing nothing, you don't understand the concept. If you are waiting for *any*thing you

are not doing *no*thing. A period of doing nothing, whether a few hours or an entire weekend, is spent time. A natural says, "Whose life is it anyway? I'm worth it. I'm not even going to see anything that needs doing, let alone be tempted to do it."

If you have to work at doing nothing you would be better off doing something.

DUTY

Anyone who recognizes a true vocation, especially at a young age (albeit later is better than never), is blessed and can make their duty their passion and pursue it with enthusiasm. Wholesome living is almost surely to result, even without great talent, excellence, or perfection.

Many devoted coaches were mediocre performers. That doesn't stop their passion for the art, the game, the science, or becoming legendary along with the success of their teams and individual pupils. Gold medal winners clearly stand on their coaches' shoulders.

EGALITARIAN

Equality between humans, by the removal of inequality, is a wholesome thing. However, to achieve equality through leveling is unwholesome and causes a great deal of mischief.

Producing equality with a steamroller is abusive. It's not nice to fool with Mother Nature and the reality is that Mother Nature doesn't distribute human traits and attributes evenly. From hair length to IQ, the distribution results in the infamous bell-shaped curve. "Children are like butterflies. They are all beautiful but some can fly higher than others."

When inequality is based on prejudice of any kind it is antithetical to wholesome living and ought to be eliminated.

EMOTIONAL INTELLIGENCE

It has been said that most of the trouble people get them-selves into comes from *feeling* when they ought to be *thinking* and thinking when they ought to be feeling. Emotional intelligence is essential to wholesome living. Almost anyone can give an impassioned speech or tirade, but as they say in AA, it isn't enough to talk the talk; you have to walk the talk.

Parents who are nearly perfect in every way, yet aren't emotionally available to their children, will be mystified when their adult children are in therapy for years, join a cult, end up in prison, or are too busy to phone or visit. They fail to see that their children are just like them, incapable of wholesome living.

Empty

Alternately becoming empty and filling up is essential to wellness. It has been said "the optimist sees the glass half-full and the pessimist sees the glass half-empty." The realist sees the glass, wonders how old that stuff is, and dumps it out.

A full glass cannot receive. Staying full gives the illusion of safety because nothing can enter and therefore nothing will change. Staying full of old ideas, judgments, and opinions is a direct route to arrested development.

To be empty, open, and receptive is to be vulnerable. As teens and young adults we work so hard at building an identity it is little wonder we cling to the identity like a drowning man clutches some flotsam or a hungry monkey grasps fruit in the vase, leaving his hand stuck inside. We need to let go, empty out, and to become at once receptive and vulnerable, to wonder who we might become if we dared to not know who we are.

ENCHANT

Enchant comes from the Latin *in* + *cantare*. It means to sing or chant. Wellness may be impossible without singing. Whether you are weary or ecstatic, if you don't know what else to do, sing. There is a song in your heart and soul for every occasion, for every mood. Look and listen for it. (Is there singing in your dreams?)

Fairies, leprechauns, unicorns, cherubs, angels, and enchanted forests are seemingly magical creatures and places that enchant. Jesus said, "Unless you become like little children, you will never see the Kingdom of God." To allow skepticism or anything else to eliminate your openness to enchantment is the worst sort of idolatry.

Opportunities to regularly be enchanted, rather, are something we should cultivate (see "Wonder"). This is at once an awful place full of suffering and a wondrous place. To see the suffering and refuse to experience enchantment would be insane.

ENDURE

Because lighthouses have endured, many people love them and want to protect them. Lighthouses have stood guard by the shorelines and persevered, often against awesome forces of nature and man, to carry out their mission of warning sailors away from danger and guiding them into a safe harbor.

Jesus also endured much because of his obedience to the Father, which is why you often find a small lighthouse standing in front of a rural church—to symbolize the prototypical lighthouse.

ENERGY

All you have to do is witness the heavy fatigue of someone who is depressed to realize that energy is essential to wholesome living. All energy is precious and, some would say, sacred. Personal energy can be surrendered or stolen. Monitoring your personal energy and doing that which is important to its generation, for example, diet, rest, play, prayer, creative endeavors, inspiration, is extremely important, as is developing the ability to focus your energy and not allow others to take it without your permission.

Energy is the light that animates. Without it we are black holes, i.e., dense and dark. It is energy that lifts a sunflower seed toward the shining sun through a crack in the shoulder of an expressway. It is energy that propels a child to go from crawling to walking. It is energy that gets us underway on our journey and results in directionality.

Wholesome living and wellness are not possible without energy. If you are a burned out star, the only alternative to a premature death is to fire up and start loving again. It doesn't matter who or what. The object of your love does not need to be worthy. It is the object that allows love to manifest and any imperfect object will do. What are you waiting for? To live without passion is idolatry.

ENMITY

Enmity is "positive, active, and typically mutual hatred or ill will." Synonyms are hostility, antipathy, antagonism, animosity, and rancor. They are a deep-seated dislike, positive hatred, hostile clash, intense ill will, or vindictiveness that threaten to kindle hostility and bitter brooding as a result of being wronged.

The reason for doing without enmity is that its hatred is likely to kill you long before it kills your enemy. The body watches the mind and when it sees enmity, it readies for war and goes to a high state of alert. When it sees enmity all the time it can never stand down. A body constantly on standby will eventually break down. As soon as possible have no enemies.

Enough

The importance of "enough" is evidenced by the frequency of its appearance in colloquialisms, e.g., "enough is enough" or "enough out of you already" or "knowing when to leave well enough alone." *Enough* implies that some requirement is barely being sufficiently met. You may be getting enough food to meet your needs but still want more. You may be getting enough love and attention to be emotionally well but still want more.

Wholesome living, which is the route to wellness, requires that you recognize what is enough. "I wish my job paid more." "Ah, but does it pay enough?" When you learn how to be satisfied with enough, anything extra can be a joy and spark your generosity. When what you have isn't enough, you've got big problems.

If someone says they don't feel like they are getting enough air, get them to a doctor immediately as getting enough air is essential to wellness. The canary the miners keep at the bottom of the shaft dies when the air goes bad. The bird's death signals that they too are already dying. The bird dies first because it is small and its rate of respiration much higher than the miners'.

If you are not getting enough in many areas of your life and you are reasonable in determining what is sufficient—good enough—for example, good enough sex, good enough food, good enough transportation, good enough housing, etc., don't sit there waiting to see if your canary dies. Time may be running out! Don't wait for your ship to come in. Maybe you will have time enough to achieve your potential; maybe not.

Wasting time is idolatry.

ENOUGH IS ENOUGH

Knowing when enough is enough is essential to wholesome living. Not knowing when enough is enough causes much grief.

Because it is subjective, no one can tell someone else when or how much is enough. Some people give up or quit easily while others don't have any quit in them. How much to take is a completely subjective determination. The capacity to abide, endure, and persevere may be an aspect of temperament and thus genetic.

When someone you are relating with evokes the "enough is enough" rule, stop what you are doing. If they are leaving, let them leave. If you corner someone who has had enough, someone can get hurt.

ETERNITY

You don't reach eternity by fastening your attention on it, but rather by living in the gift of the present. Love moves you toward eternity, but the love essential to wellness is here, now.

Eternity is not an hourglass with an endless supply of sand. If and when time ends, love will still be, and if/when you are incorporated in love you are already in forever. Eternity is eternal life in nowhere. No time, no space, no matter, nothing.

Eternity is time running but never running out; extending indefinitely, immeasurably. There is no time in Heaven. Time is planetary. Time is of the Universe not of the God above, the God of the Universe. That God is Love. Forever in Love there is no past, no future, no time. "Time makes all but love past."

ETHICS

Ethics are normative standards. They are wholesome, as far as they go. Ethics are "the discipline dealing with what is good and bad and with moral duty and obligation." Ethics are "the principles of conduct governing an individual or a group." Ethics are a good place to start when choosing the route to a graceful, elegant performance.

Ethics, like values and virtues, can point you in the right direction but why would you stop at normal, average, or the middle? Why not keep climbing? It is possible to advance to the point where you are beyond ethics, virtues, and values. They become like training wheels you no longer need. Christian mystics, Buddha, and others say it is so.

Sometimes ethics are used to defend lifestyles, like the American way, and are used to justify bombing another country into oblivion, no matter how perverted and sick the lifestyle factually is. Where is the "axis of evil?" Hell, it runs right through this country. We can hardly claim we are on the high road solely because of the initial inspiration of the Founding Fathers and the Constitution they left to guide us.

The canary has died from ethical pollution.

EUREKA

Eureka is from the Greek word *hureka*, which means "I have found." It is the exclamation attributed to Archimedes when he discovered a method for determining the purity of gold.

Finding is essential to wellness. Whether you find or not has much to do with how you look and listen. If you can't quiet your mind and focus the light that you are, like a laser, you will only pick up the noise and scattered light being pumped out by your surroundings.

Even in small cities, you can't see the stars at night. Out of fear, we light the streets, which prevents us from seeing the heavens. Light pollution. A large city is never quiet except for a few early morning hours on a Sunday. Noise pollution. If you fail to deal with the pollution of this planet you will never find (eureka!) the Kingdom of God or anything else.

A eureka-attitude promotes wholesome living. If you live heuristically, your life is a series of adventures of discovery. You learn by trial and error. Barnaby Jones, a fictional TV detective, explained he learned to play the guitar by plucking at the strings and seeing which ones sounded good together. He used the same technique in his detective work. With experience we come to know when something smells fishy or doesn't sound right. Teachers can point us in the right direction but, ultimately, it is better if we make our own discoveries (and you won't make any waiting for your ship to come in).

So, get going! Pay attention with a eureka-attitude and see what you might find. Dive into life! There is much waiting to be discovered. Go find it.

EXCELLENCE

It has been said that it doesn't matter where you are if you know the direction you are headed. This is the case with excellence. Potential and possibility only cease to exist when you are dead. Anytime prior, wholesome living involves efforts to develop potential and achieve the possible. You are invited to multiply the gifts you are given by the Universe, not sit on them like money hidden in a mattress.

Excellence, unlike perfection, is attainable. *Excellent* means "very good of its kind, eminently good, first-class." To strive for excellence is good stewardship and to invite others to try and achieve excellence is wholesome. However, to think you are perfect and talk down to others who are only mediocre is toxic. Perfectionists should wear a Surgeon General's warning on their foreheads: Warning! Perfectionist! Can be harmful to the health of others."

Unrealistic expectations are toxic. Over control and over concern with power can be dangerous to the health of others.

Combine perfectionism with Type A behavior and hostility and you end up with a lethal psychological cocktail. People with this combination not only have heart attacks, they cause them. Because they are sure they are right, need to be right, and think they are better than others, they can be violent; mean; manipulating one minute and charming the socks off you the next, all the while feeling justified; sure in the belief that their values are higher than yours. (This is not excellence.)

Sound familiar? My advice is: Be done with their foolishness. Leave before your canary quits singing.

EXCITE

It is hard to imagine wholesome living devoid of excitement. *Excite* is from the Latin word *extcitare*, which means to energize. It is not difficult to excite vulnerable people because they live exposed, open. You can excite them or rouse them to tears with any worthwhile, nicely presented sentiment.

Excitement is especially important when dealing with the armored, dispassionate, and closed-minded—the so-called hard-asses—who narcissistically plow through life like a big boat going too fast in a no-wake zone, whose captain doesn't even look back to see the havoc he has caused. It is difficult to rouse someone like this, but important to try, because of the harm they do.

Egocentric and rigid, they expect others to flex and accommodate them; but don't expect the rigid ones to be a part of any compromise. More likely their attitude is: "it's my way or the highway" or "if you don't play it my way, I'm going to take my ball and go home." Then some serious pouting that punishes others ensues.

It is difficult to abide such foolishness. "Half the cure is wanting to be cured" and these folks think they are right and everyone else is wrong. They generally don't listen, having learned all *they* need to learn. They know everything. Still, if you get the chance you should call out to them and excite them about a different way of being in the world. Their wellness and the wellness of others depends upon it.

FAITH

Faith is for beginners. With grace you can get beyond hope and faith and essentially suspend yourself in love, trust, and obedience. When asked if he believed in God, Jung replied, "I don't believe, I know." He was a pilgrim who had studied and journeyed far and wide.

When, through grace, a believer is given more than sufficient (abundant) proof, doubt evaporates and the pilgrim has the confidence and courage to see the truth, which begins to manifest repeatedly. Then honor, loyalty, honesty, truthfulness, etc., become verities. The pilgrim who acquires faith develops the quality of being true and real. This authenticity is recognizable. The absence of faith and hope is not the result of arrogance; it ensues from surety regarding the truth. With such surety comes the absence of fear and the presence of peace not typical of beginners or someone clinging to faith.

FIDELITY

The essence of fidelity is the ability and choice to be true to a commitment. Fidelity is why wellness requires being thrifty with promises. If you need to bust out and break a bunch of promises because you are suffocating, the people you promised are not the perpetrators, you are.

You can plead extenuating circumstances, but if you jump off the teeter-totter when the other person's end is high, they are going to be hurt and angry with you. Don't whine when this happens. You deserve it.

Learn from your idiocy and don't make promises you can't keep.

FLIRT

Flirt means "to behave amorously without serious intent."
There is a positive affirmative energy that is attached with
flirting. In moderation, flirting complements and is not
offensive. Flirting can promote self-esteem, which is vital to
wholesome living.

FOOL

A willingness to be a fool is essential to creativity and creativity is essential to wellness. The opposite of being a fool for love is being rigid. It has been said "Everyone knows a fool when they see one, but no one knows when they are one." This is the truth because many people live unconscious lives of quiet desperation.

Love isn't all that difficult when you get the knack of it, in fact it is a lot easier than the opposite. And part of getting the knack of love is willingly to be a fool for it. "Where would love be without fools like me?" Where, indeed? Christ was a fool for love. For us to stubbornly refuse to be foolish is idolatry.

FREEDOM

Ongoing wellness is difficult to sustain if you don't have freedom. Freedom isn't a condition; it is a state of mind. The essence of freedom is to find your own best way, undeterred by the treatment you do or don't receive from others. It is the obligation of free individuals to climb as high as they can, both civilly and spiritually.

Freedom is the absence of fear. It is associated with hope and imagination. With the right attitude a person can be free while in a brick-and-mortar prison. However, people who live in prisons built by their minds are not free—and they are dangerous. They often control others with threats and guilt. Control is on their minds. They confuse control with freedom.

The ability to imprison others has nothing to do with personal freedom.

FRIENDSHIP

During my thirty-plus years as a marriage counselor, couples have taught me the importance of friendship. Couples that are each other's best friends survive anything and seemingly everything. Yet countless couples that had everything, but were not good friends, could not manage to stay together.

It is friendship that gives us a glimpse of the dance to which God invites us. Friends are precious people. Even old rascal friends who take advantage of you and don't keep track of their obligations to you, your "Christ in his beggar disguise" friends, are invaluable.

Not all friendships are safe. Some involve a good deal of suffering. Regardless of how dysfunctional some friendships are, friendship is essential to sustained wellness. Imperfect ones will suffice. Swearing off friendship because you have been hurt is idolatry. The way out of whatever desert or dark night you find yourself in is love. Friendship. When you are hurting so bad emotionally that even breathing seems a burden, reach out in friendship and love, no matter how many times you have been kicked in the teeth. This will please God. Becoming jaundiced, withdrawn, and isolating will not.

FRUSTRATION

The essence of frustration is blocking energy that wants to flow. Although frustration is a negative reaction, it can also be a sign that various external forces are disrupting your energy. Locate the source of your frustration. If need be, get out of there before your canary stops singing.

FUN

Fun is almost always associated with laughter, amusement, enjoyment, and entertainment. The essence of fun is light-heartedness. It is gaiety and silliness. It is difficult to have fun and be serious at the same time.

Lighten up. Laughter *is* the best medicine.

Genuine

Genuine means "for real" or "bona fide." Someone who is genuine is sincere and free of hypocrisy or pretence. To be genuine requires self-knowledge. That is why when the sage was asked what the single-most important piece of advice he could give was, he replied, "Know thy self."

GET OVER IT

The ability to "get over it" is essential to wholesome living. As a matter of course, the Universe will throw you for a loop and upset you. And, if you are unlucky, your life may be like riding in a bumper car at an arcade. However, if you can't get over the bumps you will become so angry and bitter that wholesome living is soon out of reach for you.

Getting over it does not require forgiving the perpetrator, healing from the wounds the perpetrator gave you, or forgetting. *Getting over it* means moving on while not allowing the past to contaminate your future in a negative way. Certainly you will listen to the voice of experience when choices face you. Your very identity is made up, in part, by the scars, marks, and wounds you've collected as you have journeyed through life. By getting over it, you move on, with all your baggage, the best you can.

GIFT

A gift is "a notable capacity, talent, or endowment."
Synonyms are faculty, aptitude, talent, genius, and knack.
They imply "a special ability for doing something" given as a
special favor by God or nature. A gift is an important aspect
of Possibility.

To be given a gift and to recognize it, and then to willfully
abandon, risk, misuse, or abuse it rather than develop it, is
the worst kind of foolishness and idolatry, as is the exploita-
tion of someone else's gift, especially for profit.

Discovering a gift is an important aspect of stewardship.
The Universe smiles when a man or woman finds his or her
niche. Gifted people can be klutzes otherwise, but grace will
see them through if they are good stewards of their gifts.

Good Enough

Oftentimes wholesome living depends on the ability to make do, i.e., to get by happily on what you have. Learning to leave well enough alone is an important aspect of happiness.

GRIP

Being able to get a grip on one's self is essential to wellness. An out-of-control person, talented or not, who can't get a grip, is dangerous to him/herself and to others. An engine screaming out of control and self-destructing because it has become disconnected from its load is impressive—but it is still an abomination.

HAPPINESS

Like joy and peace, happiness ensues. Once you find meaning in your life, happiness follows. But, like a butterfly pursued, happiness chased, eludes. Sit calmly, breathe deeply, and the butterfly of happiness may light on your shoulder.

Endless chasing after comfort, either through obtaining pleasure or anything that reduces discomfort, is not evidence of wholesome living. It is inconsistent with the freedom that precedes true happiness.

Healing

When you learn to dance, ride a horse, climb, etc., you are going to fall and fall hard. The Universe beckons, "Come out and play," and when you do, you might trip over an unseen root and cut your lip.

If you live with openness and vulnerability, absorbingly and defiantly—"Come on, life! Give me your best shot!"—you are going to get hurt. Healing is essential if you want to restore wellness.

Healing requires intimacy and vulnerability with another person. It requires forgiveness of someone, who knowingly, perhaps with malice of forethought, hurt you.

Healing is a process, not an event you can point at. If you have injured yourself with alcohol abuse or have been hurt badly by a cheating spouse, healing will last a lifetime. We call that "recovery."

Since healing is God's business, we cannot say when it will start or when, if ever, it will be complete. We do know, however, that it does not start until the victim is ready. The truth about healing is "Half the cure is wanting to be cured."

HEAR

To hear is the ability to recognize, know, or appreciate someone's meaning. It is much more than mere listening. Just because you have someone within earshot does not mean you have a listener, let alone someone with the capacity to hear you.

To truly hear, you must convey your understanding of the sender's argument or position. However, you need not agree. To understand another's message does not require agreement. Instead it means getting it. For example, "I hear where you're coming from. If I'm hearing you right, your position on x is as follows . . ."

When someone is heard they feel located, more grounded.

HOSPITALITY

The essence of hospitality is openness. The hallmark of this openness is the manner in which new ideas and guests are received, which is invariably gently, cordially, receptively, and respectfully. Hospitable people have soft eyes and know how to provide refuge without either belittling or fawning. Hospitable people know how to be safe.

Somehow hospitable people can endure in their hospitableness in the face of all sorts of vexations, just as lighthouses do. We admire lighthouses because they are a welcome sight to sailors who need to get out of a storm. If we could endure in our hospitality as lighthouses do, we could conquer anything.

INCLUSION

Include means "to take in or comprise as part of a whole." Inclusion is the essence of hospitality. It is to wellness what exclusion is to pathology. It is the opposite of ostracizing, which is psychologically painful and dangerous. A prejudice that excludes actually assaults. To be the object of it is extremely painful and wounding.

When possible, be kind and include. That is what Jesus meant when He said, "I come as a stranger, a beggar, the least of these." He understood the play of parts and wholes. He was both part and whole, and knew it.

When you can manage it, in Franciscan fashion, sow peace and understanding, as that is the path to wellness for yourself and others.

INCORPORATED

Incorporated is essential to understanding the relationship between the parts and the whole. God's plan is the incorporation of us in Him.

God created time. The energy that started time is love. To not love, then, is to opt out of this plan. Where will that leave you?

INGENUITY

In the military, ingenuity is an important aspect of field expediency. In boating, ingenuity contributes directly to a sailor's ability to jury rig. Ingenuity contributes in the same way to wholesome living. Almost any idiot can live a wholesome life if provided with abundant food, excellent shelter, new tools, fair weather, etc.

But the day after the bomb, and thereafter, when the infrastructure is broken down, toilets don't flush, and the electricity is off, there will be pockets of people living wholesome lives. They will be the jury riggers, the people with field expediency. Their lives may not be pretty but they use ingenuity to persevere, to make do, and to carry on.

While intelligence may be genetic, ingenuity can be learned. Children who are provided with too much will not possess ingenuity. It is more likely to be found in the children of parents who were just good enough and, as a result, the children learned to fend for themselves some of the time.

Someone with an IQ of 160 and above, devoid of one iota of ingenuity, may appear dumb as a rock, while people with average intelligence who are blessed with ingenuity can dazzle others with their brilliance. Which one would you want along on a long sailing expedition?

INSPIRE

Inspire is from the Latin *in spirare*, which means "to breathe." To inspire is "to influence, move, or guide by divine or supernatural inspiration" or "to exert an animating, enlivening, or exalting influence on." It means to fill another with spirit. That is how God enlivened us, by breathing into us after He created us from dust.

If you learn how to inspire others, to light one little candle, to become one of "a thousand points of light"—a laser beam—what a gift that would be. Surely wellness would follow you all the days of your life.

INTEGRITY

The essence of integrity is boundaries. A boundary is a thin line. On one side a thing is, on the other side it isn't; like the state line between Michigan and Ohio or the hull of a submarine (air on one side, water on the other).

A loss of integrity is insidiously catastrophic. It makes wholesome living impossible.

Stay within healthy boundaries.

INTIMACY

Intimacy is a willingness to have your innermost nature be seen and tasted. It is essential to bonding and attachment. The essence of intimacy, however, is pain not ecstasy. A songwriter said, "Love hurts, love wounds, love mars." All true.

In the course of human events, hardly anything is more valuable than authenticity. Given the direct relationship between intimacy and pain, honesty within relationships is vital.

Lying to spare someone a minor hurt might seem justified. But would you ever choose to be intimate with someone who lied to you that way? If they lie to you, where will their dishonesty stop?

Intimacy is about trust. It requires vulnerability. If you say you will never be intimate until you find someone who is absolutely trustworthy, you will never be intimate. Never! Therefore, while it is prudent to develop a savvy system of determining whom you'll trust, don't proceed without a willingness to be hurt

And when you are hurt, don't whine; instead realize you are the hero, the fool for love! Where would love be without fools? Nowhere. Love could not grow without "fools" open to being hurt.

Thus it is that love is the greatest commandment and really the only one you need and why it has been said: "God loves and never truly abandons fools like these," for that is how God loves all of us.

Isolation

Much good can come out of isolation. Isolation provides the opportunity to face your self without everyday distractions. It allows you to hear the Universe whispering to you. Such retreats, like vacation and recreation, nourish a wholesome life.

IT

To have any fear or to be a mean, dispassionate, and cold person is evidence that you don't get *it*. To be needy and hoard stuff is evidence of not getting *it*. There is a special grace, elegance, ease, celebration, compassion and ready smile that ensues after getting *it*.

Indeed, "By their fruits . . ." you can spot them. Pay attention.

Journey

As anyone who has journeyed knows, "the map is not the territory" because no two people see the same exact scene, even if they are headed in the same direction and are gazing at the same horizon. It is through words and description that the part each individual *is* can move toward becoming one with the whole.

Journeys lead to new discoveries and are essential to wellness. I would rather story forth, stumble along, and traverse the rocky path, than repeat studies and replicate someone else's findings. Where is the Eureka! in that? Choose to find the truth and write your own songs about it. Ultimately that is how you will find your way.

KINDNESS

Be kind because you are, not because others deserve it. With resolve, you can be kind to the ignorant, the idiots, and the insane. If you are kind for no reason, you will confuse and inspire others. If you persist being kind in the face of adversity and hostility, you will challenge people. The cynics and skeptics won't believe you are for real.

If you can manage it, become a lullaby. This does not mean you must be a brainless, Pollyannaish airhead passing out flowers. No, you can be a feet-on-the-ground realist, albeit high on life (not drugs), who "kills" people with kindness.

Your kindness will confuse and that is a wholesome thing. As Socrates demonstrated, confusion is the first stage of learning. Oftentimes if a teacher can't confuse 'em he/she can't teach 'em.

Kindness is soothing. Given the nature of this planet, everyone needs a bit of kindness and kind people are special gifts.

LASER

You are a light bearer. The goal of life isn't to find the perfect love, it is to perfect the light that you are and become like a laser some day.

Becoming a laser—realizing and moving toward one's potential in Possibility—requires wholesome living and refinement of your light. If you scatter the light that you are all over the place, you have not yet become a laser.

Lamps and candles illuminate by casting light into the darkness. They indiscriminately scatter light in all directions. Their brightness falls on everyone and everything. The light of a laser, however, is refined. It gives off no extraneous or indiscriminate light. Its beam is focused.

There have been few laser beamers throughout history: the Buddha, Jesus, Thomas Merton, Carl Jung, Mother Teresa, and maybe a few saints. If you desire to be a laser, you would do well to consult their writings.

Letting Go

Quit controlling too much before you hit bottom. Accept that you are not in control of it all. A word of caution: letting go doesn't mean taking your hands off the steering wheel to see how well God steers or to drive recklessly because "God is your copilot." It means driving your best because you are a God-inspired driver. It means accepting that you are part of the Universe.

LEVITY

If you endeavor to live a wholesome life, you will need levity to counter the seriousness and suffering that, at times, seem to be everywhere.

Levity is an aspect of human buoyancy. Some individuals have a lot of it and are unsinkable. Others have little or none and sink like stones. The essence of buoyancy is an attitude of disrespect and irreverence. The buoyant person may appear flippant, even sacrilegious. (To the Jewish leaders of his time, Christ might have seemed that way.)

Buoyancy is a refusal to be permanently burdened by the grave circumstances that can be found almost anywhere. Without it, hospitals could not find enough people to staff their burn units and oncology floors. Buoyancy and levity are not genetic; they can be learned.

LIGHT

An appreciation of the role of light is essential to wellness, as you are a child of light. You are at once *of* the light, *in* the light, and on this planet *are* light. "Points of light," indeed.

Light is the essence of illumination.

LIGHTHOUSE

A sailor lost in the dark or disoriented in the fog sees the light from a lighthouse and is diverted from danger. In an instant he/she knows the route to a safe harbor.

There are many lessons to learn from lighthouses, which, if realized, could potentiate emotional wellness. We associate the light from a lighthouse with comfort. Its light, elevated above the surface of the water by the tower, is intermittent. It is a warning. A caution.

A flash of light gets your attention. Fireflies, sparks from a campfire, and brainstorms do, too. You have flashes of memory, flashes of recognition, and flashes of discovery. When you are awake and watchful, things light up for you. If you are asleep or too busy to notice, neither the flash of a lighthouse or inspiration can guide you or warn you.

It is not that the light isn't shining; it's that you aren't paying attention and the light doesn't register. To see light, you must become like a child in the dark, e.g., vulnerable, full of wonder, naive, wanting to be filled, and receptive.

Few see the light because they are preoccupied with success, achievement, becoming somebody, acquiring worldly possessions, life-skills mastery, accomplishments, and stuff. The advice to become like little children isn't inviting.

LIKE

Knowing what you like is essential to wholesome living. Moreover, not knowing what you like can cause all kinds of mischief, i.e., it's virtually impossible to please someone who doesn't know what he/she likes.

People who don't know what they like will be in a daze as to why bad things happen and unable to learn from their mistakes. They are at risk of being caught up in groupthink, mobs, and cults, and/or devoted followers of an exploitive leader.

LIMINAL

Liminal means "barely perceptible; of or relating to a sensory threshold." Much of spirituality remains liminal, gossamer. To hear anything you must first learn to become quiet, calm, and still. To see anything your eyes need to become like those of a child, otherwise you will only see what you have been trained to see: the consensus reality.

Important discoveries are imbedded in the liminal and God can be that way at times, alternately communicating with you boldly and brightly and at other times whispering in the low light of dusk or dawn.

You must strain to perceive Him then. This work, this leaning forward and straining with eyes wide open, may be simple—but it is not easy and not without risk. You can easily become disoriented.

LISTENING

Listening is essential to wholesome living. A good listener can help people wake up, see the light, and smell the coffee. A special listener can help you find and light the lamp that you are.

Although it is easy to teach someone how to listen it is difficult to teach someone how to hear, and beyond that, to pay heed to what they hear. Learn to listen as a gift to others, because what they acquire from your listening is self-awareness.

LONELINESS

Being able to abide loneliness is essential to wellness. To avoid the feeling entirely would be idolatry and would require compulsive flocking to be with others, non-spontaneous friendships, etc.

Crowds are not a lasting or potent solution to loneliness either. Pathetic, needy friendships, e.g., with a therapist, are transitional. Rest with your broken wings in the refuge that a good therapist offers, but remember the mission and the therapist's *raison d'etre* is for you to fly.

The essence of not fitting in is loneliness. If you are different, you don't belong. To not belong is lonely. Just because you are different doesn't make you a bad person but you wonder about it when no one wants you around. So, you learn to be your own friend and find things to do.

"Looking for love in all the wrong places, looking for love in all the wrong faces . . ." as the song says, doesn't work. Go to the mirror and see what your face has to say. Look inward, angel.

LONGING

Your capacity to tolerate longing, like your ability to put up with ambiguity, uncertainty, and constant change, is an important aspect of long-term wellness. Longing is a wholesome activity when kept in perspective, i.e., as a sort of recreation, escapist fantasy, or reverie. Such daydreaming can reduce stress.

However, when longing for something becomes intrusive, all-consuming, and results in bitterness, it is not wholesome. When longing is an aspect of obsessive compulsiveness, wellness is impossible.

The "everything in moderation" rule is especially relevant when longing is concerned. Dreaming big is not a threat, it's the not coming back to earth that is.

LOVE

Although love is often misused, abused, misunderstood, and behind a lot of mischief, love is wholesome because of its lesser-known effect on the lover. In fact, if you want the simplest guide to wholesome living, my advice would be to love everyone, everything, especially yourself—and don't stop, no matter what.

However, the majority of people think only saints can love constantly, or they plan on living that way *some day*; meanwhile they have some partying and sinning to get out of their systems. Of course, what happens is that hurts accumulate and it becomes difficult to love freely and to be vulnerable once you've been badly wounded.

Love is something you are. Perhaps you can come to this awareness by practicing loving behaviors. Certainly good works can be acts of love and build up the community, but these actions are not the love that you are (albeit they may be evidence of it). To become conscious of love as a *being* thing rather than a *doing* thing requires working toward self-understanding. With self-understanding and consciousness you can know what your intentionality is and then only intend to love.

This type of love shines on others, and is primarily mental not behavioral. It is the type of love given to one's enemies, even while in nonresistance you also give them your coat, your shirt, and whatever else they take.

MARKS

Life leaves marks. It makes lines, tracks, and wounds of all sorts. Instead of trying not to get any marks or hiding the ones you have, you ought to be proud of the dings and scratches you've acquired.

To invest too much energy in minimizing the accumulation of such marks is idolatry. And the vigilance needed to evade mark makers is intra-psychologically and interpersonally expensive and will not reduce the infliction of marks to zero.

It has been said "the truth will set you free but first it will make you miserable." And that is the truth about truth.

This planet is about suffering, and while it is prudent to not do something that is going to leave a mark, life on this planet requires coming out and opening up. Live life as if you were the biblical burning bush, i.e., on fire but not consumed by it. That way you can participate in miracles.

MARRIAGE

Research indicates that married persons live longer and are healthier than single people.

Marriage is an agreement that requires voluntary restraint; for example, restricting yourself to having sex with only your spouse. The goal of marriage is to bring two individuals into correspondence with one another. The essence of staying married is simply doing one's duty as a spouse, i.e., to be respectful, congruent, kind, true, and considerate.

MEDIATION

Mediation is a process that resolves grievances. Grievances are pathogenic. Wellness is not possible if you are nursing a grievance, or worse, multiple grievances.

Mediation is an alternative to the traditional, adversarial, so-called justice system. You cannot stay well for long if you are embroiled in a conflict that comes to the attention of our criminal justice system. To be addressed by the criminal justice system is the equivalent of a soldier entangled in concertina wire with a flare igniting overhead, i.e., you are in a world of hurt. Wellness is not possible. Be still until the flare goes out and then crawl out of there before your canary dies.

MEDIOCRE

Mediocre gets a real thrashing by perfectionists but, when you think about it, it isn't half bad. *Mediocre* literally means "halfway up a mountain." Therefore mediocre is halfway between good enough and excellent (perfection isn't attainable and to think you have attained perfection is idolatry). Yet we use *mediocre* as a pejorative, for example, "his writing was just mediocre." If mediocre means "ordinary" or "moderate ability," mediocre writing ought to be good enough not to obscure the message.

Good communication is essential to wellness. If people don't communicate out of fear their speech or writing is only mediocre, wholesome living will not be possible. The Greeks said, "In the middle is virtue" and that is where moderation is. Being mediocre is pretty good.

MINDFULNESS

Mindfulness is an antidote to distraction and the route to mindfulness is paying attention. A distracted mind is like being in a room with many radios turned on high volume, each tuned to a different station. The planet is a noisy place—and so is much of the solar system. Paradoxically, when the Universe speaks to us, it whispers. If you do not deal effectively with the noise you cannot hear the Universe.

A few gifted individuals can mindfully do several things at once but most of us can barely chew gum and walk at the same time or play the radio and drive.

Distraction and the operation of machinery is dangerous; but distraction with resultant failure to hear the Universe is idolatry.

MISTAKES

Does everything always work out for you? If you aren't making any mistakes, maybe you are not developing your potential at a reasonable rate. If you've never failed, you have been a poor steward of your time and talents.

The goal of life is not to avoid mistakes and to never fail, it is to advance in understanding and wisdom. You don't do that by avoiding. The goal of life is proficiency, not perfection. The pursuit of perfection is hubris, idolatry, while the pursuit of excellence is at once admirable, reasonable, and attainable.

To make children afraid of making mistakes ought to be a felony offense. There is no better way to steal many positive accomplishments from a child's future than by making him/her fearful to try anything. Life is like climbing a sand dune, i.e., three steps forward, slide back two—but you can make it to the top. Even when you make mistakes, keep climbing.

MODERATION

Wholesome living is associated with moderation. (As the Greeks said, "In the middle is virtue.") Sometimes though, even in a wholesome life, it may be necessary to visit extremes, for instance, in emergencies, on adventure vacations, or for amusement. But staying in an extreme situation for any duration rules out wholesome living.

Wholesome living is associated with balance, consistency, and moderation. The goal of wholesome living is to thrive, not merely survive. And thriving is essentially ruled out by extremes of anything.

MORTIFICATION

Mortification is an antidote for hubris. It means "the subjection and denial of bodily passion and appetites by abstinence or self-inflicted pain or discomfort; a sense of humiliation and shame caused by something that wounds one's pride or self-respect." The "everything in moderation" rule especially applies to mortification. A little of it or just enough to keep one grounded is a good thing.

MUCH OBLIGED

"Much obliged" is at once a salutation and recognition that you are in someone's debt. Wholesome living is impossible if you refuse to keep track of and own your indebtedness. Wellness depends on individual responsibility, especially owning the consequences of your actions.

When people are irresponsible in this regard, they are the first to blame others for their situation. "My life, the way I feel, everything, is the way it is because of you." "If only you would support me unconditionally I would exit my misery." In their self-absorbed concern with the dramatic and tragic in their own lives they always take the victim position and never see their indebtedness to anyone.

As Jesus said, "They can see the sliver in their friend's eye but cannot see the beam in their own."

MYSTERY

An appreciation of the mysterious—what is, has been, and will be unknowable—is essential to wholesome living. The sage asked, "Is life a mystery to be lived or a problem to be solved?" Of course, if sustained wellness is the goal, balance between these two is the answer.

Failure to appreciate mystery often results in anxiety, worry, and fear of the sort ancient sailors had when they thought the world was flat and they imagined what would happen if they sailed too far and went over the edge. Not only is ". . . the future not ours to see" there are many things we can not know without supernatural help while we are held down by gravity in the physical body in time and space.

You need to learn to be content with heading in the right direction and less concerned with making record time. You will know soon enough where the path leads if you stay on it. To not stay on the pathway is idolatry.

The weaver of dreams and the weaver of the Universe remain a mystery. We can peer into it and appreciate how some of it works, like Jung did. But don't think too much. It is not wholesome.

NATURE

Nature is where the external truth of God exists. Communing with nature is advised by most wise people, like Voltaire's retreat to the garden, Thoreau's retreat to the woods, and St. Francis' rapport with creatures.

It is sometimes human nature to be needy, greedy, jealous, envious, and paranoid. The redeeming aspect of our nature is our capacity to love, not contractually (although that is better than not loving at all), but to covenantally love others as God loves us.

NEEDS

Needs are the physiological and psychological require-
ments that must be met for your well-being. There are
several hierarchies of need, stretching from those essential
to survival to those required of an ordinary citizen, to those
of someone who occasionally has peak experiences to sainthood and enlightenment (like the Buddha or Jesus).

However, meeting your needs does not guarantee wholesome living and wellness. Ignore your needs at peril, but to
"become all you can be," to achieve your potential, requires
awareness that goes beyond meeting your needs. You can
have everything you need, but with a bad attitude you won't
amount to a hill of beans. Such foolishness is the worst kind
of idolatry.

OPEN

To be open means to be unobstructed, unconcealed, unconfined, and undefended—it is the ability to form spontaneous and unguided responses, to be fully observant and discerning.

Nothing thrives in a pressure cooker. If you remove the lid or leave the weight off the vent in the lid of a pressure cooker, pressure will not build up, even if the fire underneath is quite hot. It is the same with people. When people become closed, bottled up, and constricted, pressure begins to increase. Their breathing will become shallow, non-rhythmic, and more rapid than normal.

You can survive in a fortress or refuge, but you cannot thrive there. A cave can protect you from falling rocks, but it is not an environment conducive to wholesome living. To live in a wholesome way you have to open up and come out of your cave.

If your life has contained much adversity and hurt, and you have had to hole up repeatedly, in order to come out at all, you must first put on your armor. This is the psychological equivalent of the armor that knights wore to protect themselves when jousting. Such armor has its limits though because it adds weight. Too much armor and the knight can't find a horse strong enough to carry him.

People employing what Freud called "body armor" are in the same fix. Once you put it on and feel more safe as a result, then it is difficult and requires a great deal of daring and courage to take it off, to open up, to come out, and to become vulnerable.

A refuge remained in too long becomes a tomb. If, due to the wall you have built around your heart, you cannot be hurt, then you cannot be intimate, reached, or touched either. That is sad and not wholesome. Staying open means remaining capable of being hurt, which is a good thing.

Opportunity

Opportunity is "a favorable juncture of circumstances." Such a juncture, which sometimes presents itself as the proverbial fork in the road, seems to often occur serendipitously.

You cannot determine when opportunity occurs due to chance, chaos, or order, or whether it is luck or grace. In the second half of life, given that love is centripetal, it is a good idea to view every opportunity as an act of grace. To refuse to do so would be idolatry.

OTTER ATTITUDE

Otters are God's way of manifesting the optimal ratio of work to play. Otters are efficient, effective swimmers and skillful predators; therefore they don't need to worry about where their next meal is coming from or what they will use for shelter, since it seems any hollow log will do. Every day otters spend a large portion of their time playing. They are very social and call out to each other as they slide down a clay bank into the water, scramble up the bank to slide down again, etc. Their attitude seems to be that "a day without play is a day without sunshine."

How many days in a row have you gone without playing? It has been said: "All work and no play makes a dull boy" and that's the truth about the ratio of work and play. Develop an otter-attitude toward life. When it is acceptable and appropriate to make your work playful and fun, do it. It promotes wellness—just as a sense of humor does.

Own

To *own* means "to confess, to acknowledge; to get a grip on what you've done." At first blush, this might seem simple, but to own requires first never to lie to yourself and then to not lie to another.

Radical getting a grip on what you've done and owning it means not attempting to justify your actions. This is especially the case if your action (or lack of action) hurts someone or results in some sort of wreckage.

This sort of owning requires fearlessness because it excludes lying to avoid upsetting someone. Such courage and honesty often result in a good slap alongside the head.

PARTICIPANT-OBSERVER

Participant-observer is the name of a model of conducting phenomenological research. The researcher at once participates as one of the subjects and observes the others and him/herself as a subject in the study.

This is also a good way to live because it promotes wellness. *Participate* means if you get invited to dance, then dance. Then, observe. Observe others, but, more importantly, also observe you.

Disengage from your mind, your body, and your feelings. Tell your ego to button its lips so you can open your mind, suspend judgments and identifications, and bring new eyes to your observing, looking on as though you were seeing the activity for the first time. Forget everything you think you know about this phenomenon. Interview yourself: "What is going on here? What is this?"

If you practice this often enough, eventually you will light up with recognition. "Ahh, this is . . ."

Passion

Synonyms for *passion* are *fervor*, *ardor*, *enthusiasm*, and *zeal*. They mean intense emotion, compelling action. One's passion can go over the top and be ungovernable or it can be balanced, energetic, and unflagging.

Nowhere is moderation more helpful than with passion. Overreaching passion usually leads to disaster. If you can't control your passion, it will control you, which isn't wholesome. On the other hand, a life devoid of passion, without enthusiasm, would be idolatry. To put your passion in a box and lock it away is not the route to wellness.

Psychological repression, suppression, and sublimation lead to transmutation, which means the energy (of passion) exhibits itself in a disguise, sometimes as great art, music, a poltergeist, or fetish. Best to keep the beneficent devilish energy that passion can be in front of you.

PATIENCE

The impetuousness of immediate gratification ("I want what I want when I want it") is inconsistent with wholesome living. Patience is preceded by calm. Patient individuals take time to contemplate the cause of their suffering and to bear up under it.

Since patience is a virtue, it is impossible to be too patient. However, patience has to be balanced with a reasonable assessment of how things might change. If it is clear a painful situation will never change, even the most patient person is released.

Patience can avoid or reduce the escalation of suffering. To not fume at the imposition of pain caused by some other's inconsiderate, perhaps unconscious, act or failure to act, should be expected only of those approaching sainthood.

And, while we are endeavoring to advance in patience, it is not fair to expect patience from others when we inadvertently, albeit being true to ourselves, rain on their parades.

This is an increasingly crowded planet. Most family groups live in less than expansive homes. We are going to bump into each other, step on each other's toes, etc. It is unavoidable.

To promote patience and tolerance is wholesome; sustained wellness is not possible these days without it.

PAY ATTENTION

If I could say only two words about wellness they would be "Pay attention!" Pay attention to everything and everyone—even the dull and ignorant. They may have a story to tell. If not, move on.

To grow in wisdom you must pay attention—be aware, take note. "Make haste slowly" as you story forth. Be gentle. Tread lightly.

"The goal of life isn't to find the perfect love, it's to perfect the love that you are."

PEACE

The essence of peace is the absence of enemies. To be at peace for any length of time requires staying out of disputes and having a strong resolve to seek reconciliation rather than remain in conflict with others.

To live in peace means avoiding contentiousness, harsh speech, discord, and all but minor disagreement. Peace is harmonious.

Peace is interrupted by contestation. Peace will not prevail when there is an ongoing struggle over power or contests to see who will be in control.

Peace is essential to wellness. To experience peace, even briefly, intermittently, is a major accomplishment. To have peace ensue in a sustained way, as a result of your practice, is through grace at once an awesome blessing and an imitation of Christ.

Peace confounds people who would be your enemy. When they endeavor to get you all wrapped around the axle and you remain at peace they will want to know the truth that you know.

Not only can allies live in peace, enemies can too—if they respect one another, reconcile, and agree to "fight no more, forever."

Actually, peace is rarely tried by anyone. How many married couples live in peace most of the time? Peace excludes the bickering that is typical of American couples, which periodically blows up from daily quarrels and disputes into chaotic emotional turbulence that oftentimes includes verbal or physical abuse.

Tranquility ensues from peace and cannot continue to exist without it. Perhaps that is why it's so rare.

PERSPECTIVE

To say dismissively, "Our differences are just a matter of perspective," i.e., no big deal, reflects a failure to appreciate how huge a matter perspective is. To speak of perspective diminutively is idolatry and any sort of idolatry is risky business.

As long as you are going to risk having an opinion, taking a stand, giving others your "take" on something—do it boldly, own it as yours, identify your authorship (perhaps it is uniquely yours, if so copyright it!)—that way you have a better chance of learning something.

It is irresponsible to fail to identify and own one's perspective. Everyone "reads between the lines" but how many realize that when you read between the lines, what you read is what you wrote? It's okay, even important, to take a stand, to give something a personal slant—but initial it.

PERSISTENCE

Persist means "to go on resolutely or stubbornly in spite of opposition, importunity, or warning; to continue to exist, especially past a usual, expected, or normal time."
Persistence is what we admire in lighthouses. They endure.

Keep on "keeping on."

PERSPIRATION

Perspiration and hard work are part of wholesome living. Sustained wellness cannot be achieved without physical and mental effort and the resultant perspiration.

Perspire is from the Latin words *per*, meaning "through" and *spirarae*, meaning "to blow, to breathe." Respiration + Inspiration + Aspiration = Perspiration.

Through hard work the spirit can move toward Possibility. If you keep moving, a collision with Possibility is unavoidable. The time and place are up to the Universe. To persist or not is up to you.

PLAY

A day without play is like a day without sunshine. Many people work seven days a week, month after month . . . and then take a vacation. Such a work-play cycle rules out wholesome living—and the vacations often turn out to be disappointing disasters.

The reason so many vacations are disastrous is they are too infrequent and extravagant. People get run down and then expect a vacation to rescue them. Big vacations are stressful. People try to cram a year's worth of play into two weeks. Foolishness. The essence of vacation is vacating, i.e., "Adios. I'm out of here!"

You can mix work and play, as long as there is enough play with no work mixed in. In wholesome living, work punctuates play, not the other way around. Play is restorative, cheat on it and you get sick. Don't play and you will pay.

Living a wholesome life requires maintaining a balance between work and play. Play has many forms, but the quintessential common denominator is its re-creative quality. Work disguised as play, e.g., golf, doesn't meet this requirement. "Play golf" is an oxymoron. Tournament fishing doesn't make the cut either. It is work. Work discharges your batteries; play recharges them.

There are two kinds of gardeners, those who work in the garden and those for whom gardening is playing in the dirt. Look at the gardens; even the plants know which is which. Plants thrive for people who play amongst them. There is a direct correlation between a green thumb and play. "The Universe is unfolding as it should." Figure it out and plants will thrive for you.

PLEASANT

Pleasant people, with their pleasing and invariably gentle ways of being in the world, balance out the anti-wellness impact of their vexatious opposites. *Pleasant* means having qualities that tend to give pleasure; having or characterized by pleasing manners, behavior, or appearance."

Being a pleasant person isn't the first order of business—knowing thy self and being authentic is.

However, after you've achieved that, being a lullaby to others is a good thing.

PLEASURE

While it is true that pleasure and the relief of pain are the roots of most addictions, the solution is not a life devoid of pleasure. That would be idolatry. Pleasure is to be enjoyed in moderation.

Yes, you can overdo a good thing—and you should—once in awhile. Would Jesus wear a Rolex? Probably not. Would He laugh at a wedding guest whose heart was gladdened by a little too much wine? I think so. Would he approve of too much of that? No. Jesus frequently advised maintaining a heightened state of consciousness, staying awake, keeping your lamp full of oil (not booze), and burning brightly.

Don't sleep the stupid sleep that ensues from an addiction. A little wine at bedtime to help you relax and get a good night's sleep is not inconsistent with wholesome living and wellness. (There is even scientific evidence that alcohol in *moderation*, is good for the heart.)

Pleasure contains other traps for the unconscious or otherwise unwary pilgrim. One such trap is the belief that because of a particular set of values and virtues you *deserve* the pleasure you get, or worse that because of *how* you live you don't deserve any suffering the Universe may assign you. This kind of thinking is at once hubris and idolatry.

If, as a result of luck and/or grace (one cannot always tell when luck is the result of intended grace or just an ol' planetary windfall produced by random chance), good planning, preparation, talent, opportunity, timing, good decision making, discipline, or hard work, you arrive at a place where some of the attributes are pleasurable, enjoy the heck out of it—but don't flaunt it. While you may have earned it, give *many* thanks and don't get trapped in the delusion that the abundance you have is because you deserve it.

There were certain things even Jesus couldn't abide. Hypocrites were one group, maybe hubris in His name will be another.

POTENTIATE

Wholesomeness ensues when certain conditions are met. Learning how to potentiate these conditions, i.e., making them more likely to happen, can accelerate the onset of wholesome living.

The route to wholesome living will sometimes be direct, but because it is the outcome of many things, more often you will not be able to go there directly from where you are, rather you will have to position yourself in a location that is en route to wellness. For example, you may have to retrace some steps or regress before you can actually progress.

Going backward is challenging and may sorely test your patience; just like getting a backlash out of your fishing reel so you can resume fishing or untangling the kite string from a tree so you can have the joy of sending the kite soaring once again.

PREPARATION

Preparation needs to be handled with care and used in moderation because it is *future* oriented. Life is lived in the *now*. Life isn't preparation for a test or final exam. It is not a dress rehearsal. This is it. (St. Francis wouldn't soak beans overnight for tomorrow's soup. He felt doing so was over-concern for the future.)

Preparation is prudent yet optional. Life will present you with experience, whether you are prepared or not.

With luck or grace you might stumble into success without preparation, but don't bet on it.

Rapport

In relationships where rapport is achieved, there is harmony, conformity, accord, and affinity. To be a safe person for others, you need to know how to establish rapport. To understand someone, requires rapport.

Perhaps the essence of rapport is a matter of pacing, of getting in sync with another. It is falling in step, a particular kind of joining that results in "singing on the same page in the hymnal" to produce harmony.

Relationships devoid of rapport lead away from wellness.

READINESS

The route to readiness begins with awareness, which is waking up to what's happening around you. If you are inattentive and self-absorbed, you won't have a clue about the people and events in your life. Readiness is essential to wellness.

RECONCILIATION

The goal of reconciliation is to free yourself from the shackles with which your sin has burdened you. To knowingly fall from the grace of another is the worst sort of idolatry.

If you have alienated someone, the process of reconciliation is probably more difficult than you think. It isn't enough to acknowledge that your wrongdoing hurt the person. It isn't enough to say, "Let's forgive and forget." That is incomplete. To reconcile means to restore to friendship or harmony.

Name your offense. Name and own what you did.

To offend someone and not get caught may spare you the hurt their awareness would bring, but it offends the Universe and does not let you off the hook. *You* know. You need to go to that person and tell.

Sneaky sins that you get away with do the greatest harm to you, because eventually you have to balance the pain it will cause the person, if you tell them, when you want to be free. If the truth will hurt them too much, it may be a greater sin to tell them what you did and got away with.

Once you are face to face with your victim, you are obligated to help them understand. You need to explain as much or as little as you know about your offense. Answer all their questions (their questioning may last for months). They may ask: "How could you do this?" or "Why did this happen?" They will need to situate themselves in your story.

If, however, you cannot do this without lying, don't go. Learn how to tell the truth first, because if you don't, your efforts to reconcile will make the situation worse and hurt your victim even more. Share everything you know about your self, which may account for your behavior.

Then they'll need to decide what to do with the rest of their life given that this has happened. They may need to do extensive damage control. You are obligated to drop what you are doing and help them with this. If you must, attend therapy sessions with them—and don't be bitter about it. You did this to yourself. You have no one to blame but you.

Go in love and peace. And, above all else, do no more harm.

RECREATION

The essence of recreation is not entertainment, thrill seeking, or extreme sports. A recreation area should be quiet, peaceful, and serene. (Noisy off-road vehicles and recreation areas are mutually exclusive.)

The consistent laser beamer has learned what cycle of rest and play is optimal. The light in you, like the lighthouses of bygone days, cannot burn brightly without constant tending. (This is the essence of admiring lighthouses.)

What charges your battery? You must find out what works for you. It will involve some combination of rest and play.

REJECTION

Being able to abide rejection is essential to wellness. (Ask any successful writer!) The essence of rejection is the decision by another to not affirm something you assumed. To avoid the issue of rejection, don't assume anything in the first place!

Then, when something nice happens to you unexpectedly and unanticipated, you can have the experience of being delighted, which is the essence of joy. Whereas the confirmation by another of something you assumed, is a slippery slope leading to smugness.

Therefore, eschew praise and know that blame is evidence of some other's discontent. (If they never did *content* they couldn't have the experience of *dis*content.)

RELATIONSHIP

It has been said "man needs others to become himself" and "it takes two to see one." As a result of these truths, relationships are essential to wholesome living.

Relationships can be long-term, short-term, or transitory. They are essential to becoming and establishing your particular way of being in the world.

REPEATS

Repeats are important opportunities for wholesome living. Many things are repeated: dreams, words, phrases, etc. You need to relax and open yourself up to these repeats. Calm down, become quiet, and be receptive. It's like turning on your computer to see if you have any messages. If the Universe says: "No unread messages," you can return to what you were doing. But if something is repeated, yet again, duplicate the process and pay attention.

You should appreciate the opportunity to deepen your understanding of any phenomena that continually presents itself to you. Realize that the Universe will give you the same experience over and over again until you recognize it for the first time. Repetition is the mother of knowledge.

RESOLUTION

Resolution is one of the few exceptions to the general principal that wellness results from living in the *now*. Resolutions are forward-looking and future-based. They are important to wellness because a resolution is reached by a series of progressive steps that leads parties in a conflict or state of alienation to a solution. If you are locked in a dispute with someone, better to reach a compromise, resolve the issue, and move on.

If you can live wholesomely and happily without it, simply walk away. To persevere in trying to fix the unfixable may be courageous, but it is also insane and idolatrous.

RESPECT

The essence of respect is the ability to see another and to recognize the worth of that person; acknowledging they are "a child of the Universe" and "have a right to be here." Respect should be given for no reason. It should be given to the dumb and ignorant, for they too have a story.

The essence of respect is seeing another being, there, just as they arc. Respect does not come in degrees. Below a certain threshold, it simply doesn't exist. Above that threshold, it is fully present. There is no such thing as half-assed or grudging respect. Respect, like honor, must be given fully and freely.

To gaze at a person with respect is not to approve of their style, deeds, and so forth. It is the action of seeing them there. Respect is an aspect of self, given to another unconditionally. It is time and energy expended, conscious of the larger miracle in which it is imbedded.

Respect is devoid of a design or protocol to change. Respect and an agenda for whittling on another are mutually exclusive. Respect, rather, means starting where the other is.

REST

If you are going to live enthusiastically, which is the essence of wholesome living, you must rest. Rest big or briefly—but frequently. *Rest* is short for *restoration*.

Wholesome living involves the discharge of energy in the form of light, and recharging one's batteries. To be a star requires periodic rest. If you are discharged and exhausted all of the time, you are a black hole. No light escapes from a black hole.

Rest and play are not the same thing. You can rest without play and play without rest. Play without rest is re-creative but not restorative. Rest without play is restorative but not re-creative.

The knack of combining the two is essential to wholesome living.

REVERIE

Reverie is an aspect of pace. Pace relates to how you "do" time; it is an aspect of style. *Style* can be defined as "what you look like doing some thing."

When someone enters reverie deeply, the passage of time drops out of his/her awareness, just as it does when an athlete goes into the zone or a gardener gets into the flow. A person comes out of reverie and might realize the better part of a day has gone by unnoticed, and more than one obligation has come and gone. That is a reason to gasp and sigh—but not to conclude that time has been wasted.

Reverie used as a pejorative is evidence that someone doesn't understand what this place is, what is going on here, and the mechanics of how it all works.

Jesus knew what he was doing when he chose fishermen to be his disciples, to be "fishers of men." True fishermen have a demonstrated capacity for reverie.

Ruth

The essence of ruth is compassion for others and sorrow over your own faults. *Compassion* means to suffer with and to understand the suffering of another. If you are one hundred percent successful in escaping suffering, it is a result of ruthlessness.

SADNESS

The cost of denying sadness that results from the losses you suffer is prohibitively expensive and, over time, rules out wellness. The fear of sadness disguises itself as a determination not to give in to inane, insipid, or banal sentimentality. However, it is impossible to live like this for any length of time and still have dignity, grace, mercy, class, and elegance. These qualities come from surrender, which is accepting this planet as it actually is, i.e., a gossamer mix of love, fear, loss, ugliness, acquisition, beauty, suffering, and joy.

If you trust the process, sadness yields to grieving, and grieving to letting go. Wholesome living requires that you become good at shedding tears; good at sadness; and good at joy; of celebrating with tears what is being accomplished, the possible, the opportune.

SAFE

Becoming a safe person is a gift to others and potentiates wellness. Becoming a safe person is simple enough, but not easy. Teaching another to be a safe person involves much instruction in *not* doing, because the essence of being a safe person is *not* harming, and the quintessential feature of being a safe person is *not* being afraid.

Here are the Dos & Don'ts on becoming a safe person:

Don't judge.

Learn how to hold a person without touching them.

Learn to hover.

Pay attention.

Learn to open up the other person.

Develop soft eyes. Don't stare. Do not look only into the other's eyes. Breathe with them.

Don't be in it for anything.

Trust the Universe.

Start out with the assumption that you don't get to *keep* the person, i.e., ships sail into and out of a harbor's refuge.

Never lie.

Share the truth as you know it.

Listen.

Look at a person and be silent.

Don't *want* anything from someone.

Wait.

Don't teach if instruction is not requested.

Forget what you believe and don't know.

Be present.

Experience the other person, walk in their moccasins.

Do not think.

Do not lead.

Do not follow if the person leaves.

Invite. Welcome.

Trust that the other can find his/her own best way, just as you found yours.

Forget about right or wrong.

Make haste slowly.

Be patient.

Do not be concerned with results. Do not have any goals.

Be curious. Allow.

Be serious in a playful way.

Get in the way of inspiration.

Be non-reactive ("Well, are you just gonna sit there?" "Yes." "Aren't you going to do something?" "No.")

Be thankful that the person is there, whether you are being sent to them or they to you; initially you cannot tell and right then it doesn't matter.

Forget good or bad, right or wrong—just see.

View life from the other person's perspective.

Be awake with this person, right now.

Observe.

Don't talk about people who aren't present.

Don't have anything to say (no canned speeches).

Be spontaneous.

Do not resist.

See the person first; the doing/action will take care of itself.

Be safe for yourself.

Forget outcomes.

Don't have a story to sell; don't look for a story to buy.

Don't hold any viewpoints.

What you love you want to last, but it doesn't; what you hate you want out of our life, but it doesn't go.

Be careful.

Let go of doubt and belief.

Don't look for something to like . . . or notice anything to loathe.

Don't have opinions.

Don't try to talk the person out of anything.

Don't see conflicts as problems; see them as opportunities for growth.

If you are a damned fool for love, how bad is that?

Know that time is something you are in, not something that you are; so don't worry about it.

Conflict isn't an accident; it is an assignment.

Linger awhile.

Think how much you would regret if your arrogance led to anger that hurt any creature. Be patient.

Know that if you hold a person, at some point you'll have to let go.

Own your wants, wishes, desires, and intentions.

Do not project.

Be passionate.

Accept consequences but do not blame.

Know your heart is a mansion with many rooms and faster than you can put new names on doors, it expands. There is always room at the inn.

Sauntering

Pace has a direct impact on wellness. It is no wonder that as improvements in technology speed up everything in our daily lives, people get sicker. It is impossible for mankind to adapt to the pace of modern life, because the changes have occurred too quickly.

It wasn't long ago, before the relatively recent invention of the steam engine, that the fastest mode of transportation was a good horse (or a bicycle without brakes headed downhill). Sprinting to escape danger or to improve cardiovascular fitness, and brisk walking for exercise or to get out of a cold rain is allowed, but should only be done in moderation.

Sauntering is the pace of wholesome living.

SAVOR

Savor means "to relish, to delight in, to enjoy." The essence of savoring is in evidence when someone stops to smell the flowers.

Wholesome living depends on good nutrition, exercise, avoidance of toxins, and daily sanguine sauntering during which you can savor the stars, the sunset, the flowers, and the fresh air.

Scruples

Scrupulous means having moral integrity and acting in strict regard for what is considered right or proper. People who are scrupulous are honest and just. They behave honorably and conscientiously.

However, being over scrupulous is a form of idolatry. Being over scrupulous alienates others because it breaks the Thirteenth Commandment: "Do not judge," which includes judging yourself too severely.

Easy does it with scruples.

SELF-RESPECT

Wholesome living is impossible without self-respect, which is vital to self-understanding. Seeing yourself as you actually are, results in your self-esteem and self-respect being independent of what others say you are. This essential I *am-ness* is the basis of great vitality and aliveness.

SENSES

The five senses make important contributions to our well-ness. It is with our senses that we perceive the phenomenal world and, like St. Francis, see evidence of God in His creatures. God gave us senses so we could go on journeys of discovery and with our potential in Possibility, discover Him.

It is with our senses that we perceive the evidence of God.

SERENDIPITY

Serendipity is defined as the faculty of making fortunate discoveries by accident. I think serendipity is one of those things God uses to remain anonymous. So many important medical discoveries have been serendipitous.

To trust in serendipity then, is not foolish. Rather it is evidence of a deep conviction, based on experience, that if we live with optimal attitudes what we need will appear. Serendipitous living requires openness to Possibility. An individual who is rigid and has mental adhesions and hardening of the attitudes cannot live wholesomely.

Being open to serendipity means staying open to the possibility that a so-called windfall is actually a personal blessing, encouragement, or confirmation that you are on the right path.

Serenity

Wellness cannot be sustained without at least episodic bouts of serenity. The essence of serenity is calmness and tranquility. It is not a goal or an end in itself. It can only ensue.

Serenity, like happiness, if pursued, eludes. You cannot go directly to serenity. It is an outcome of wholesome living.

But don't pray for serenity, pray for things that potentiate it, like courage, authenticity, meaning, and vulnerability.

SIGH

Pay attention to your sighs and the sighs of others. Sighs are clues about how your spirits are; monitoring the condition and level of your spirits is essential to wellness.

Some sighs are pregnant, like the sighs of someone who loves you when you haven't figured it out yet.

Tune into sighing. Hear it as a song not a complaint. Sighing is music. When you hear someone sigh, ask yourself, What song is playing? The Universe at once hums, groans, and sighs. Can you hear it?

SILLY

What a joy it is to see children being silly and laughing
with delight. Being silly is a lightheartedness that is defiant
given the nature of this planet and what is going on here,
e.g., capital punishment, wars, hurricanes, AIDs, etc.
Silliness is a levity that defies the gravity of our situation.

SIMPLE

Simple is associated with wisdom, as in "Keep It Simple Stupid." *Simple* means uncomplicated, being free from guile, vanity, ostentation, or display. Simplicity is essential to wellness.

However, simple is not easy. For example, Christianity, when boiled down to its essence, is simple—but that does not mean easy, which is why Christianity has never really been tried by more than a few people at any one time.

Here is a challenge: Forget any and every instance in which someone hurt you or stole from you. Just let go of it. Simple? Yes! Easy? No!

SIN

Wholesome living is difficult if much alienation exists. If your goal is to never intentionally alienate, you must pay attention to sin. It is the awareness of and the appreciation for the negative impact of sin that keeps you on track.

Sin divides and causes estrangement. Anything unnecessarily divisive is idolatry. It is much better to build a bridge than to dig a divide.

It has been said, "Sin is the foolishness we do to ourselves." Sin is one of those additives in life you do better without. Who but a fool unnecessarily causes alienation or lives alienated?

To monitor sin effectively you must understand perception. You must be able to see yourself as you actually are.

SONG

Life is song. It is music. Invite others to sing along with you. Sing as you paddle; whistle while you work. Hum a tune.

If your song has only one note, know that is all you need when you are surrounded by an orchestra—and you are!

Sing. Sing. Sing. To not sing, to not dance, is idolatry.

SPACE

An appreciation of space is essential to understanding the Spirit and to not dance with Spirit is the sort of poverty that rules out sustained wellness.

Steven Hawkins (and others) tells us that when space and matter are compared, there is much more space than matter. Watch a lighthouse. There is much more time between flashes than time occupied by flashes. Try and anticipate the flash of a lighthouse and you will see this reality. You will need to pay attention to the space between the flashes if you want to capture the lighthouse in a photo. You would do well to live like that, to pay attention to the space between things

SPIRIT

Spirit means "an animating or vital principle held to give life to physical organisms." It comes from the Latin *spiritus*, which means breath. Good breathing is essential to wellness and maintaining constant awareness of your breath is wholesome indeed.

Stay in the Present

Being unable to stay in the present is a disability that rules out sustained wellness. Look not at what you know, watch rather for what you have never seen. That is the naive way and it is how you can see the Kingdom of God.

Don't look for what is *not* in the moment; watch for what appears in it. A relaxed driver, free of assumptions about the road ahead, is a better driver than a fearful one who dreads a stretch of road with scary features, thinking "When I get through this boring stretch or these hills and curves, everything will be all right." That is as bad as driving while looking in the rearview mirror. You are not fully present.

STEWARDSHIP

Stewardship means "the individual's responsibility to manage his life and property with proper regard to the rights of others." Good stewardship also means managing your time and talents in a way that maximizes beneficial outcomes. Wellness for you (and the entire population) is not possible without stewardship.

STILLNESS

Stillness is essential to seeing clearly and seeing clearly is essential to wellness. The sage said, "Muddy water let standing still becomes clear."

This is the truth about what the Greeks called *epoché*. If you learn to quiet yourself you may be left with just the sound of your breath and your heartbeat. You ought to be able to do nothing, to think no thoughts, and feel no feelings. Stillness is right now, it is nothing.

SUCCESSIVE APPROXIMATION

When people try to "get it" all at once, suffering often ensues. Sometimes big chunks of learning occur (they are described as epiphanies, gestalts, or awakenings); however they usually follow much successive approximation. Successive approximation recognizes and builds on the "one step at a time" and "a journey of a thousand miles begins with a single step" theories.

We crawl before we walk. This too is recognition of successive approximation, which is reflective of our developmental nature imposed by the Creator. We arrive on the planet as infants rather than being deposited here as full-grown adults.

"First things first" recognizes successive approximation and is good advice.

SURRENDER

Letting go, surrendering, is essential to wellness. *Surrender* does not mean passive. You can be at once surrendered and proactive. If someone starts to beat you with a stick, you can take the stick away. However, if you then begin to beat your perpetrator with the stick you have exited surrender and gone to war.

The surrender of wellness is not surrender to an enemy, it is the opposite of idolatry, it is surrendering to the Universe, to a higher power.

Know that grace is real, that the Universe cares for you and wants you to live in trust, love, and obedience.

SYNCHRONICITY

Carl Jung defined synchronicity as "the seemingly acausal juxtaposition of events." To dismiss the meaningful juxtaposition of events in all instances as mere coincidence is to try and live a wholesome life without an important guidance system operating.

You might do all right because we are blessed with redundancy in guidance, just like a modern jetliner has more than one way to find an airport. And while navigating through life with synchronicity as our only guide might be a hoot, it is an important augment to more salient indicators, which can confirm we are making a correct course change or warn us away from a dangerous, ill-fitting, or wrong path.

Thus, attention to synchronicity can steer us around obstacles and help us avoid the need to retrace our steps later due to error.

TEACHER

Good teachers are essential to wellness. A good teacher is someone who prepares and helps you during your life journey. Sometimes the best teachers don't have a degree in education.

THOUGHT-STOPPING

Being able to stop unwanted thoughts is beneficial to wellness. Like a parent stifles unruly children, we should be able to say, "Do something about that noise. Stop!"

Thought-stopping techniques involve commanding your thoughts to stop or at least to pause.

Obsessions (unwanted intrusive thoughts) are terribly disabling. I have never met an obsessive, compulsive, or obsessive-compulsive person who could claim to be well.

The brain isn't malicious; it just prefers to be busy. If you fail to teach your brain to think in a disciplined way, it will think away the livelong day. You should be able to apply the "enough is enough rule" and say, "Shut up, mind" and have it stop.

THOUGHTFULNESS

Thoughtfulness is a state of being alert. It is the opposite of recklessness and carelessness. It is the opposite of the proverbial "loose cannon." Indeed, rather than endangering others, thoughtful action or inaction is based on a concern for others' needs or best interests.

The essence of thoughtfulness is heed. When you pay heed to someone you are giving them the beautiful gift of attention.

TIME

Wellness is not possible without an acute appreciation of time. Time is not an enemy that works against you, nor is it an ally on your side. Time just *is*.

The truth about time is that it is a structure you are in, and you ignore it at great peril. You don't spend time, it spends you—eventually it will expend you. There is no such thing as wasting time. What's wasting if you are ignorant about time is your life. Therefore, be sensitive to time.

Hear the clock tick. Burn brightly. If you can, be a beacon for others. Illuminate. When you "dance like nobody is watching" you are an inspiration to others, a candle brightly shining in time.

TRANQUILITY

To experience tranquility means you are free from agitation of mind or spirit and free from disturbance or turmoil. A tranquil person is unvarying in aspect, is steady, stable, and relaxed; though not necessarily passive.

Tranquility is a life-long challenge that begins at birth and precedes all of the many other things essential to wellness. Learning to still one's mind and to quiet one's self is an aspect of wholesome living absolutely essential to wellness.

Here is the progression:

self-control = awareness = tranquility = ease = wisdom = second naivety = seeing the Kingdom of God.

Transparency

Transparency of an authentic person, i.e., someone free of duplicity, is associated with peace, wisdom, and wellness. You develop transparency by practice, practice, practice. If you are a liar, the protocol is to quit one lie at a time and "don't quit quitting." If you wear many masks, the protocol is to discover them and discard them one at a time until there is only one you. Then in true humility you can say, "I am what I am and that's all that I am." You own all that you are and all that you are not. "What you see is what you get."

Transparency is at once outrageous and refreshing. One of the many benefits of becoming transparent is never needing to be ashamed again.

TRUTH

Just as climbers ascending a mountain know there are different avenues leading to the summit, there are many routes to truth. Regardless of which path you take to the truth, once you've attained it, it is the same.

You are unlikely to be alone when you find the truth. When others see what you have (mostly freedom and fun because the truth sets you free), they will either want what you have or attack you because you frighten them.

UNDERSTAND

To understand is essential to becoming. It literally means to stand under. If you have ever stood on someone's shoulders so you could peer over a wall, you are familiar with the essence of being stood under; and if you have ever lent your shoulders to that same endeavor you know the essence of standing under.

Most advances have come as a result of a present-day rescarcher standing on the shoulders of yesterday's pioneers. The best teachers gladly lend their shoulders to their students and experience joy when the students regularly surpass them.

UNDERWAY

When you are underway, there is Possibility. Follow your bliss. Pursue your dreams. If you're lost in the clouds, try to fly out of them by climbing higher.

Your wings are the spirit of inspiration, aspiration, and perspiration (work). Use your wings to get underway, to spiral higher and higher, with an open heart and an open mind that asks, "What's this?" with enough trust and obedience to accept that what you are presented with is no accident and courage to keep going, to stay underway, when your masterpiece isn't finished and your tools are worn out, as long as you are still breathing.

There will be plenty of time to rest when you are underground. As long as you are above ground and able to see the sunrise, get up and get underway.

Vacation

The essence of vacation is vacating your usual haunts and doing something different than the daily grind—or doing nothing. Big vacations (like Disneyland) are okay—but have little to do with wholesome living. Entertainment and amusement are *elective*. They are not essential to living well and can even be antithetical from a wholesome living viewpoint.

The vacating of wholesome living and the stereotypical American vacation have little in common. Joining thousands of others on crowded highways, where rage manifests regularly, is hardly wholesome.

Today a trip to a so-called wilderness area, wildlife refuge, or national park is likely to involve hoards of people, shuttle buses, and evasive maneuvers to stay out of others' home videos. These vacations may be worthwhile, even uplifting, but they have little to do with wholesome living. If you want to work at such a vacation, no problem, just don't forget to rest and play before you go and after you return.

Wholesome living requires *daily* vacating and, given the way our culture is set up, more serious vacating once a week when the weekend arrives.

VALENCE

Valence is a measure of your capacity to unite, to react, and to interact. If you were alone on an island, valence wouldn't be much of an issue; but in this crowded society it is. As you move along your path, assuming you have found it, you will come close to or collide with other people. You have valence and they have valence.

Valence is encountered as a force as you wrestle with directionality. Wellness requires that you see and understand your path so you can return to it when you collide with someone with the wrong kind of valence for you.

An awareness of how valence operates potentiates wholesome living.

VALIDATE

Validate means to affirm or confirm. The fact that so many people grow up unaffirmed is one of the major reasons wellness is not more widely distributed in the population.

Too often validate does not mean affirm your feelings by empathetically acknowledging them in a reflective way. Some people are so wounded that *validate* means "support me, come to my defense," even when I'm wrong.

Value

Determining value is how we establish whether a relation-ship or an activity is worthwhile. Value isn't always easy to see or determine. Someone else's folly may turn out to be invaluable later on. Whether or not something is pure fool-ishness depends on its source, i.e., on what is being expressed, on what is manifesting.

That is why it is said, "By their fruits you will know them." A tree in the orchard that never bears fruit is hoed and fer-tilized one last time (and perhaps put under duress and shock); then, if it doesn't produce, it is cut down.

To grow in value is the way to appreciation. Strive to be useful. If you are a singer, sing. If you have a green thumb, feed others and give them flowers for their table.

Variety

Variety is an antidote to sameness and boredom, which can be lethal to wellness and wholesome living. It has been said, "Variety is the spice of life." Sameness is unexciting.

This planet is a sampler. A disinclination or outright refusal to try anything new is a tragic disability. By comparison, people who can dive in and sample life in all its abundance are truly blessed.

Vector

Vector means a quantity that has magnitude and direction. As you move through life, you are a vector and you intersect with other vectors, either moving or at rest, like pool balls. Sustained wellness is impossible if you wander through life willy-nilly. And if your wandering gets manic or urgent, it is not wholesome. Your canary will quit singing and wellness will erode.

In the course of human events, wellness is less likely to exist if vector and valence are left to chance. Staying on course requires both backbone and steering. If you passively sail downwind, you cannot determine where you will end up.

You must stand up for something and watch out for what you fall for, that is set sail and like Ulysses don't fall by being lured into any traps.

Virtues and Values

Virtues and values are guidelines to wholesome living and wellness. Science indicates that it is unlikely we were deposited on the planet with a complete set of virtues and values intact. Virtues and values evolve by paying attention to see what works, to what has a pleasing outcome.

Virtues and values are like rungs on a ladder. Once you climb up the ladder, if the ones below you were to become unavailable, it wouldn't be a problem unless you planned to climb down, and who would want to do that?

VULNERABILITY

Vulnerability does not mean being a doormat or standing by passively as some mean, wounded, or unconscious person hurts you or others. When your canary quits singing, get the hell out of there.

Being vulnerable doesn't mean being helpless. You are not a helpless captive of your past.

Vulnerability is an openness to being fooled. To be a fool for love is the highest calling. There is no foolproof guide for navigating love. Why go then? Because ships might be safe in the harbor, but that's not what they are built for. As Jung said, "Safety is a devouring goddess," and his is the voice of considerable experience.

You can trade the experiences of joy and intimacy and meeting someone for safety . . . the truth is, that is not what we are made for. We are not made to be so safe and so sound that when we fall we won't get hurt. To go high is to jump out over the abyss, as if the Universe will grab us by the hair if we begin to fall. Sometimes the Universe will and sometimes it won't. When it doesn't, we hurt. It has been said without such hurts, "the heart is hollow."

It would be naïve in the extreme to expect to experience intimacy and be spared any hurt. To wish for safety, to press for protection, is prudent; but to expect it would be indicative of someone who has not been paying attention to what is happening on this planet.

To be vulnerable in a relationship means capable of being hurt. Sometimes by someone who has hurt you once or more times already.

Be careful with whom you are intimate. But if you opt for safety rather than vulnerability you cannot see another and you cannot see yourself. To truly become who you are, vulnerability is essential. If you can find safe people to be vulnerable with, that is prudent, but if you can't find safe people, what then? "Love the one you're with."

To not love, no matter how good your excuses are, is idolatry and that is the worst sin, resulting in the greatest alienation of self, from self, and from others.

"It is better to have loved and lost than to not have loved at all." Are there rewards other than potential intimacy, joy, wonder, and timelessness? (I say "potential" because as Aquinas said, "First we leap, then we know.") Yes. The most valuable potential reward for being vulnerable, for being a fool, is the spread of love. As the songwriter said, "Where would love be without fools like me?" Where indeed! Nowhere.

WANT

Knowing what you want is essential to wholesome living. If you want to advance in self-knowledge, which is necessary for wellness, you have to dare to know what you want and what you like and don't like.

WHIMSY

Too much gravity is not wholesome, and when it is chronic, wellness is ruled out. *Whim* means "a capricious or eccentric, often sudden, idea or turn of mind." Whimsy is a wholesome defiance to gravity.

Too few people allow whimsy free play in their lives. It is good to live ready and willing to respond to an irrational or unpredictable idea or desire. The science of love is whimsy.

WILD

It is a great oversimplification to say that wild is bad and tame is good. Things that are wild are robust, adaptable, and have stamina. These are wholesome traits.

When the "wildness" gets refined out of plants they begin to require special conditions or they don't flourish. They can't adapt. They die out.

You must be respectful regarding the natural unrefined wildness of your nature.

WISDOM

By developing wisdom you will find the truth, and seeing the truth is essential to wellness.

It is not typical of wise persons to be anxious. It is typical of wise people to own their childishness and the ability to make a fool of themselves.

It is not typical of wise persons to have regrets, desire, pride, admirers, or attachments. Wise people do not seek to tame wild things; they seek to tame themselves.

The calmness of a wise person is not affected by either praise or blame.

It is typical of a wise person to build up this planet rather than cling to it.

A wise person is not greedy, agitated, envious, avaricious, deceitful, or miserly. A wise person does not spread disinformation.

The wise person is patient and harasses no one, hurts no one, and finds fault with no one.

Let go of winning and losing.

Give freely and have ill will toward no one.

See your duty and do it, giving freely.

WONDER

Wonder is the quality of exciting and amazed admiration, it is to feel curious or in doubt about something. Wonder potentiates wholesome living via its role in creativity.

Wonder and intellectual curiosity are essential to new discoveries. To wonder with an open mind as things manifest themselves moment-to-moment is to participate in the energy of the Universe; the energy of us.

To wonder at the marvel that another is, with no thought, nothing to offer them, nothing to want from them, is to put yourself in the way of a miracle.

Words

We use words to symbolize and communicate meaning, to express or describe an experience. We use words to convey meaning in a relationship, and wellness and wholesome living depend on meaningful relationships.

Wellness would be difficult without words, whether communicated by speech, Braille, Morse code, flags, etc. It has been said that man needs others to become himself. We need to be present to one another and then stay connected in a communication loop. Words can cause a lot of trouble, but we'd be in more trouble without them. Wholesome living depends on communication.

WORLDS

There is the world that I am and my environing world;
and there is the world that you are and your environing
world. It is not possible to truly share these worlds. When we
meet and face each other, our worlds are governed by the
limits of time and space. But when we truly meet in love, a
supernatural, "non-local" world of no time, of spirit, that
already contains us and started time for us, joins us, and
then we are together forever because "time makes all but
love past."

That is as good as we can do on this planet. Knowing we
can do it and doing it as often as possible potentiates our
wellness and heals others.

WORTHY

To be worthy, one must have integrity. A person who does not have integrity is not safe. It has been said, "By their fruits you will know them." This is true of worthy persons. Persons of worth honor others, and you can feel it.

Wholesome relationships can only be had with people worthy of us.

WWJD
(WHAT WOULD JESUS DO?)

The Universe sends many teachers who invite us into their tents for lessons: Carl Jung, Buddha, Jesus, B.F. Skinner. Our job is to pay attention, to look, to see, to listen, and to hear. It isn't to imitate and live in our time as they lived in theirs.

We are not born with an operator's manual; but if we look and listen the Universe's teachers will provide us with directions that enable us to go where Buddha went for enlightenment and where Jesus went to be one with Abba.

YEARN

Identifying what you yearn for and desire is essential to wellness. It is unhealthy to not know what you want and, sometimes it requires courage to identify and admit what you yearn for.

Yearning is related to longing. We can long nostalgically for something we had in the past. Yearning is tender, softer, and warmer—more like a sigh—than longing is. You can yearn for something you've never had.

Yearning is future-oriented. Whereas longing often involves looking back and comparing now with then, yearning looks forward and compares what's missing now with some imagined future. We long backward and yearn forward.

There is no point in running hysterically or manically after what you yearn for. As Buddha advised: "Become still, empty. The spirit that made everything out of no thing will come and light on your shoulder." Any urgency reflects a misunderstanding of grace. If you chase after grace, it will elude you. If you remain peaceful, an angel will remain with you and provide whatever teaching or consolation you need.

Pray for meaning. Pray for courage and instructions. Peace and serenity are the "prize."

ZEST

Zest means "a quality of enhancing enjoyment." Zest is the spice of life; it is to be savored. To not delight in zest is idolatry. A willful refusal to savor so much of God's creation that is "piquantly pleasant to the mind" is the worst sort of foolishness.

Zest is a key ingredient in the formula to wellness.

God gave us our senses to find our way home. It is difficult to imagine His being pleased by any effort we make to disable our senses.

AFTERWORD

WELLNESS RELATES TO NUTRITION, EXERCISE, access to health care, avoiding toxic physical and psychological environments, and limiting exposure to even mild vexations to an absolute minimum.

Ultimately, however, wellness arises from within, as a result of making the ego an employee rather than the employer, and living in the gift that is the present, while also acknowledging that the past, present, and future are seamless.

Everyone living has a horizon. Tomorrow contains today, but today does not dictate the shape or content of tomorrow. The realities of today do not predict the novelty of tomorrow. Possibility ensues from but is not limited by today.

To live with hope is not foolish; it is realistic. Although to expect is unwise and all problems begin as assumptions, living with openness and expectancy is often rewarded with new discovery and opportunity.

To truly hope is not to pray for relief from suffering, rather it is to trust the Universe, evolution, and the resultant uniqueness of tomorrow.

Wellness has nothing to do with being an earthly or planetary success. What the Universe considers a successful life may or may not be reflected in planetary success.

When I'm asked to give a single piece of advice on wellness I say: "Pay attention while regularly creating a space for others and give them the gift of your presence now, in this moment."

ABOUT THE AUTHOR

T IMOTHY J. UHLMANN, Ph.D. is a fully licensed psychologist. He currently directs the Wellness Program and Behavioral Health Department for six federally qualified health centers (Michigan Primary Care Association Affiliates) in Michigan's northeast lower peninsula.

In the 1970s, Dr. Tim was one of the pioneers blazing the trail for open adoptions and in the 1980s he oversaw the resettlement of seventy-two Vietnamese children from a refugee camp to new homes in northern Michigan.

In 1987, after sixteen years in child welfare, Dr. Tim established a private practice, specializing in marriage and family counseling.

On September 12, 2001, he began a foray into "Primary Care Medicine." In the fall of 2004, Dr. Tim graduated from a three-year spiritual director program presented by the Dominican Center at Marywood in Grand Rapids, Michigan.

Dr. Tim is a rural psychologist who resides on a lake in northern Michigan with his wife, Gloria, two dachshunds, and the lighthouse he built in response to 9/11. Its "Limited light is dedicated to the unlimited light of God."

He can be reached via e-mail at drtim@straitsarea.com and by writing to: TJU Publishing, P.O. Box 244, Topinabee, Michigan 49791.

COURSE INFORMATION

Dr. Tim Uhlmann's Grief Works course will be available in 2005. This course can be adapted for large or small groups and can be varied in length.

Grief Works can be targeted for different subjects, i.e., wellness, chronic illness, weight loss, depression, spiritual growth, life style changes, etc.

If you are interested in having Dr. Tim present a Grief Works course in your area, please contact him at:

TJU Publishing
P. O. Box 244
Topinabee, Michigan 49791
E-mail: DrTim@freeway.net

INDEX

To ORDER COPIES OF

When Your Canary Quits Singing contact:

TJU Publishing
P. O. Box 244
Topinabee, MI 49791
E-Mail: DrTim@freeway.net
www.doctortim.biz

Purchasing Information:
  $ 12.95 U.S. / $17.95 Canadian
  plus $4.00 for shipping and handling

Send check or money order made payable to: *Dr. Tim Uhlmann*

Discounts available for bulk orders.

Dr. Tim is available to speak at seminars. Contact him at:

TJU Publishing
P.O. Box 244
Topinabee, MI 49791
Telephone: 231-597-9743